Cooking
Greek

cooking greek

A Classic Greek Cookbook for the At-Home Chef

Pemi Kanavos with Tanya Stamoulis

Worldwide Greeks
Boston

Dedication
This book is dedicated to Kostoula Panagopoulous, Georgia Kanavou and Lena Athanasiadis.

Thank you for teaching us what Greek philoxenia is and instilling in us our love of Greek cooking and feeding others.

ISBN: 979-8-9873181-3-3
Imprint: Independently published

Art Director:
Pemi Kanavos

Editor & Content Director/Creator:
Tatiana Stamoulis

Developmental Editor:
Katherine Tsoukalas

Digital Marketing Expert:
Nick Stamoulis

Taste Testers:
Dionysis Aggelakis, Akis Stamoulis, Leo Stamoulis

Published by: Worldwide Greeks
www.WorldwideGreeks.com

contents

My name is Pemi Kanavos, and I am excited to share with you my love of Greek cooking. I learned in the typical way that most Greeks do - from family - with recipes, methods, and techniques being passed down through the generations. I am also a classically trained pastry chef. It has been a joy to put these recipes together for you.

I've always been proud of my Greek identity. Even though I grew up between the United States and Greece, Greece has always felt like home to me. It's a feeling I can't really put in words. A feeling of belonging and a sense of calmness envelopes me when I think of the land, the sea, the culture, the people and the food. My mother's beautiful village, in particular, fills me with nostalgic pride. This is where I would spend my summers as a teenager.

The beauty of having roots in a Greek village is that it is a place to not only holiday but also reconnect with family and friends who do not live close by. I would count down the days for school to be over so we could leave Athens and head to Messinia on the southern tip of the Peloponnese. I would reunite with my family and friends from both Greece and Boston and there would be lots of hugs, kisses (one on each cheek as is tradition) and tears of joy. The summer was always full of laughter, good company and of course great food and plentiful wine. My grandmother, as are many Greek yiayias, was the heart and soul of our family. She would cook traditional dishes for us like Pastitsio, Gemista and Youvetsi, all accompanied with fresh bread she would bake daily for us in the stone oven.

In Greece, there are an abundance of ingredients that are grown and produced locally which heightens the flavors of the food. The olive oil we used was harvested from my grandmother's grove. It was so fresh and pure that when you tasted it, it started as a tickle and turned into a slight burn in the back of your throat. The eggs were gathered daily from a chicken coop in my grandmother's back yard. I have a vivid memory of her cracking open one of the fresh eggs. I had never seen such a bright colored yolk in my life. It was that day that my curiosity for food and flavor was born, and it was in her tiny kitchen that my passion for good food, family meals and feeding others blossomed.

In Greece, people love to eat, and what they love even more is eating together. We love to share our meals and feed others. We are social and hospitable and love the concept of Mezze, or shared plates. This is the case not just for dinner, which was the norm in my Boston-based years, but for all meals. In Greece, we share breakfast, lunch, dinner, dessert, and of course, coffee. It's the norm and speaks to the generosity of Greek hospitality or filoxenia which is a core value of the Greek culture.

Greeks are very generous people who would, quite literally, give you the shirts off their backs. Even though the younger generation has not seen too many hardships in their life, our cherished patriarchs and matriarchs have come from humble beginnings and have faced many hardships. Despite what they have gone through, they live their lives to the fullest and are very appreciative of what they have. Their lessons on life and their resilience are things that I have tried to adapt in my day-to-day as well.

My parents came from the same area in Messinia, though not from the same village. They are very proud of their heritage, and have passed that pride down to my brother and me. Even though we lived a good part of our childhood in the United States, our parents worked hard to ensure we grew up with a strong sense of identification with our Greek culture, language, heritage and cuisine.

I remember being enrolled in Sunday school at our church to learn about the Greek Orthodox religion and the afternoon Greek school in order to learn the Greek language and history. I hated waking up and going to Sunday school every week, or missing out on playing with our big wheels in the backyard with our friends three times a week in order to attend Greek school. But looking back, I have to say that it was the best gift my parents could have given me. The gift of reading and writing in Greek has given me a deeper understanding and connection with my heritage, and this helped me in my transition when we moved to Greece.

Growing up, my mother would cook traditional Greek recipes for us daily and host many gatherings. She would always cook enough food to feed a dozen people, and leftovers were always turned into lunches. Having Moussaka for lunch (or 'moose-caca", as parodied in the movie "My Big Fat Greek Wedding"), was an everyday normal meal for me. Over the years through all of our family gatherings and daily dinner table, I came to understand and admire the importance of food and feeding others. This notion of feeding others was even further reinforced when I moved to Greece at 8 years old. It was my first time witnessing a Greek Easter feast in the village. Preparation for this feast started days in advanced culminating into the celebration of Easter Sunday. All the traditional foods of Easter were displayed on the table and enjoyed not only by the family, but also by villagers that would come by to give their Easter wishes. Even if they weren't hungry the guests were invited to taste everything on the table.

I started shadowing my grandmother and mother in the kitchen, picking up knowledge as the years went by. They taught me most of what I know about Greek cooking. They were both remarkable cooks, and not because they had gone to a top culinary school or apprenticed under a culinary master, but because they cooked straightforwardly and from the heart. They cooked seasonally with ingredients that were harvested from their own backyards.

I always loved creating food and feeding my creations to others. My first job creating food was at my family's restaurant in Boston, where I worked through my college years. It wasn't until then that I truly realized how important it was to preserve the food I grew up eating. I would call my grandmother and asked her how to make Pastitsio or Tzatziki and wrote them down so I could replicate them later. This is when I realized how difficult it was to follow a recipe from Greek women

who cook using their senses. Greeks don't cook using strict measurements. My grandmother and mother always would say "Bale me to mati", which literally translates to "add with the eye". Making these dishes took some trial and error which I documented along the way until I perfected them. Eventually I formalized my passion for cooking by earning a Culinary Arts Degree.

Years later I found myself living back in Boston with my own family and "torturing" my son the same way my parents "tortured" my brother and me - by sending my own child to Greek school. While waiting for him during classes, I met some like-minded and amazing women who became my Greek village. One of these women, **Tanya Stamoulis**, along with her husband Nick, turned their passion for preserving Greek heritage, culture, language and cuisine into multiple websites and forums including **WorldwideGreeks.com**. It was in the basement of a Greek Orthodox church, waiting for my son to finish classes, that I first dared to share my dream of writing a cookbook. I'm so happy that I did, because years later it's finally happening. Tanya and I were able to collaborate on something we are both passionate about: Greek cooking and helping to preserve the traditions and culture of Greece.

I can't begin to express the thrill I feel when I'm in the kitchen. Preparing any meal is exciting to me, but preparing these nostalgic Greek meals gives me great joy. Planning out an elaborate meal and whom to invite to share the meal with me makes me happy.

This book is my way of sharing the beauty of Greek cuisine as well as teaching and preserving it for all of you to enjoy. It humbles me that I can share with you what I hold dear to my heart: "my recipes", recipes that have been passed down for generations and will continue to be passed down for more generations to come. Thank you, and cheers to more culinary adventures to come. **-Pemi Kanavos**

mezze

What is Mezze, Exactly?

In the Greek culture, mezze is an important part of culinary traditions. It is a collection of dishes that are meant to be shared. In some cultures these are referred to as appetizers, but for the Greeks mezze is an experience. Although mezze can be enjoyed as a snack or appetizer, it is very frequently treated as a full meal.

Family and friends gather to leisurely enjoy these shared plates, often pairing them with wine or other local Greek spirits such as ouzo. The tradition of mezze actually dates back to Ancient Greece, where it was against the law for bars to provide customers with alcoholic drinks if they weren't also eating.

The term mezze is more conceptual than about a set menu of foods. Anything can be served as a mezze, as long as it's served on little plates and garnished for presentation. How it is served is just as important as what is being served. Some common dishes include pita bread, stuffed grape leaves, fried meatballs, dips and spreads.

Mezze Table Staples.

Greek olives are a necessary addition to any mezze spread in Greece. You have the option of marinating them or serving them garnished. Olive oil should be drizzled over the dish before adding fresh herbs, orange zest, and chopped garlic. There is no standard marinated olive recipe. The majority of people use the ingredients they already have on hand.

Greek cheese is incredibly diversified, yet few people outside Greece know this. Whatever type of cheese it may be, it is a wonderful complement to the spread! Whether you have feta cheese, mizithra cheese, soft goat cheese, or kefalotiri, it all works. A flat platter with olive oil, cheese, and chopped fresh herbs from the garden is a typical presentation method for cheese.
Dried herbs like thyme, oregano, or dill are frequently used instead of fresh herbs when they are not readily available.

Greeks view bread as a symbol of friendliness. It is also the most basic kind of mezze that is offered. People often place a plate of fresh or toasted bread on the table when guests arrive at their home or take a seat at a restaurant or bar as a "welcome gesture". Of course, it goes beyond just goodwill, they anticipate you eating it as well! Frequently, a little pitcher of olive oil will be included with the bread, so you can generously drizzle it on as you choose.

Dolmadakia
Stuffed Grape Leaves

mezze

MAKES 30 PIECES

INGREDIENTS

8 ounces jarred or fresh grape leaves

½ cup olive oil

1 large onion, diced

3 spring onions, minced

¾ cup uncooked, short grain rice

¼ cup vegetable stock or water, or more as needed

Juice from 1½ lemons

½ cup mixed finely chopped parsley, dill, and mint

1¼ teaspoons salt

¼ teaspoon pepper

Lemon wedges, to garnish

INSTRUCTIONS

Place the grape leaves in a pot of salted boiling water and blanch for 1-2 minutes. Remove them with a slotted spoon and transfer them to a colander to drain.

Meanwhile, in a large saucepan, add ¼ cup olive oil and heat over medium-high heat. Add onions, spring onion, and sauté until softened, about 2 minutes. Add the rice and sauté for 2 more minutes. Add ¼ cup of veggie stock and half of the lemon juice and stir.

Lower the heat and let the rice simmer for about 3-4 minutes until the rice has soaked up all the liquid. Remove the filling from the heat and let it cool down for at least 10 minutes. Add the parsley, dill, and mint. Season the filling with salt and pepper.

ASSEMBLY

Lay 4-5 leaves on the bottom of a large pot, depending on the size of the pot. Use any ripped or broken leaves. This bottom layer of leaves will help prevent burning or sticking of the stuffed leaves that will be placed on top. Place a grape leaf on your working space, stem side facing toward you and dull side facing up. Place 1 tablespoon of the filling on the bottom of the leaf. Fold the edges inward and roll it up. (Do not roll too tightly as the rice will swell and break open the leaf).

Place rolls side by side, in the pot, seam side facing down. Do not leave any gaps. When the first layer is complete, continue with a second and/or third layer. Add the rest of the olive oil, lemon juice and enough stock to cover them completely.

Place a plate over rolls with the back end of the plate facing you. This is done to keep the rolls in place while cooking and to prevent them from opening. Cover and bring to a boil. Reduce the heat and simmer over a low heat until the rolls are nice and tender, about 50 -55 minutes.

Try one roll to make sure that the rice has been cooked sufficiently and the leaf is tender. When ready remove from the heat. Allow them to cool in the pot, uncovered. Serve at room temperature or cold in a serving plater.

Tzatziki
Cucumber Yogurt Dip

mezze

SERVES 6-8

INGREDIENTS

1 large hard English or hot house cucumber, peeled, halved, and seeded

¾ teaspoon salt

3 cloves garlic and more to taste

16 ounces full fat Greek yogurt

3 tablespoons red wine vinegar

⅓ cup extra virgin olive oil

INSTRUCTIONS

In a medium bowl, coarsely grate the cucumber either by hand (box grater using the large holes) or in a food processor fitted with a coarse grating disk. Sprinkle salt over the grated cucumber, stir and set aside so the cucumber can release its liquid, about 20 minutes.

Peel the garlic and cut the cloves lengthwise and remove the green sprout in the center. Crush and finely mince the garlic.

In a large bowl, combine the yogurt, garlic, vinegar and mix until well combined. Set aside.

Give the cucumber a good squeeze over the sink to remove most of the water - do not rinse. Stir the drained cucumber into the yogurt.

Add the olive oil in 2 additions. Mix until well combined after each addition. Taste and adjust salt, garlic and vinegar if necessary. Cover with plastic wrap and refrigerate overnight for the flavors to blend. The longer the garlic rests in the yogurt, the less sharp the bite it will have and the better it will taste. Serve in a small bowl and drizzle with some olive oil. Serve as a dip or a sauce for your Souvlaki or grilled meats.

Notes: The yogurt used needs to be the Greek strained variety so the tzatziki remains firm and dense. It is very important to squeeze the cucumber and remove all of its juices. If this step is omitted the cucumbers will release their juices into the tzatziki, making it very watery. The green sprout from a clove of garlic can make the garlic taste slightly bitter. Removing it retains the pure garlic flavor.

WorldwideGreeks.com **favorite**

Tirokafteri
Spicy Feta Dip

mezze

SERVES 8-10

INGREDIENTS

2 roasted red peppers, cut in small pieces

1 tablespoon vinegar

½ cup extra virgin olive oil

Chili pepper, to taste

16 ounces feta cheese, finely crumbled

⅓ cup Greek yogurt

INSTRUCTIONS

Add the red pepper, vinegar, olive oil, and chili pepper to a food processor and blend for 1 minute. Add the crumbled feta cheese and yogurt and process until the mixture is fairly smooth and creamy. This should take about 1-2 minutes.

Transfer the mixture to a serving dish. Taste and adjust the seasoning, if necessary. Smooth the top and create a few swooshes with a spoon. Top your dish with additional chili flakes (depending on how spicy you want it) and a light drizzle of extra virgin olive oil.

Refrigerate for at least 1 hour. Serve this with crusty bread, pita chips or as part of a larger platter.

WorldwideGreeks.com **favorite**

Taramosalata
Greek Caviar Dip

mezze

SERVES 8-10

INGREDIENTS

14 ounces white stale bread (crust removed)

1 small onion, grated

3 ounces jarred tarama (carp roe)

⅓ cup water

¾ cup extra virgin olive oil,

2 tablespoons lemon juice (freshly squeezed is best)

Toasted pita chips or bread, for serving

INSTRUCTIONS

Soak the bread in water and squeeze well to remove the excess water. Coarsely grate the onion either by hand (box grater using the large holes) or in a food processor fitted with a coarse grating disk. Let it drain in a colander.

Add the onion, tarama (roe), and 2 tablespoons water to a food processor and blend until creamy, about 2-3 minutes. With the motor running, add about half of the olive oil in a slow steady stream. Add lemon juice, bread and rest of the water. Add the remaining olive oil in a slow steady stream, as if making mayonnaise. Process until the mixture is very smooth. You may need to add some more water to loosen the mixture, if the mixture gets too thick. It should be the consistency of a velvety hummus.

Transfer to a bowl and cover. Refrigerate for at least 2 hours before serving. To serve, spoon the Taramosalata in a wide, shallow bowl.

Smooth the top and create a few swooshes with a spoon. Drizzle with olive oil just before serving. Serve this with crusty bread, pita chips or as part of a larger platter.

Notes: This spread can be made 1 day ahead and refrigerated in an airtight container. For a lighter version, add ½ cup olive oil and ¼ cup sunflower oil. Tarama, or Greek caviar, can be found in Greek food markets and some fish and specialty markets.

Melitzanosalata
Eggplant Dip

mezze

SERVES 6-8

INGREDIENTS

6 eggplants

2 cloves garlic, finely minced

½ medium onion, finely chopped

2 tablespoons apple cider or balsamic vinegar

Juice of half a lemon

¾ teaspoon salt, plus more to taste

¼ teaspoon freshly ground pepper

⅓ cup extra virgin olive oil

2 tablespoons parsley, finely chopped

2 spring onions, thinly sliced (including the green parts)

2 roasted peppers, finely chopped (optional)

Fresh herbs (parsley, chives, etc.), to garnish

INSTRUCTIONS

Preheat the grill on medium heat.

Pierce the eggplants in several places with a fork to allow the steam to escape while cooking. Grill the eggplant for about 25-30 minutes.

Turn frequently until the skin is evenly charred all over and softened.
Let the eggplants cool down.

When the eggplants are cool enough to handle, cut them in half and scoop out the flesh and any remaining flesh from the skins. Discard the skins and remove as many seeds as possible from the flesh. Place eggplant flesh in a colander set over a bowl. Let it drain for 15-20 minutes.

While the eggplants are grilling, yåou will prepare the rest of the mixture. Add the garlic, onion, apple cider vinegar, lemon, salt, pepper, and olive oil to a food processor and pulse until well blended. Add the flesh of the eggplant and pulse 3-4 times. Transfer the eggplant mixture to a large bowl and fold in the parsley, spring onions, and roasted pepper (if using).

Cover and refrigerate for at least 2 hours. Ideally, refrigerate overnight so the flavors can blend together. To serve, garnish with fresh herbs of choice, drizzle on some extra virgin olive oil and taste for seasoning. Serve this with crusty bread, pita chips or as part of a larger platter.

Notes: You can also broil the eggplants about 8 inches from the heat for about 30 minutes or place the eggplants on a sheet pan lined with parchment paper and cook for 40-45 minutes at 400°F.

If you want to turn up the heat on this appetizer, add ¼ teaspoon (or more) red pepper flakes with the garlic and rest of the ingredients.

Look for very firm and heavy eggplants with green tops. Darkened topped spongy eggplants are not fresh and will have a bitter taste.

Keftedakia
Fried Meatballs

mezze

MAKES 20 MEATBALLS

INGREDIENTS

1½ cups diced, day old bread (crusts removed)

1 cup milk

1 pound ground beef

1 cup onion, finely grated

1 garlic clove, smashed and minced

1 egg

1 tablespoon mint, finely chopped

2 tablespoons parsley, finely chopped

1 cup olive oil

1 tablespoon salt

Freshly ground pepper

Flour, for dredging

12 lemon wedges, to garnish

INSTRUCTIONS

Soak the diced bread in the milk for 5 minutes. Squeeze bread dry and discard the milk. Place in a large bowl. Add the ground beef, onion, garlic, egg, mint, parsley, 3 tablespoons olive oil, salt, and pepper. Mix gently by hand until all the ingredients are completely combined. Cover the bowl with plastic wrap and refrigerate for half an hour.

Form into little meatballs, doing your best to keep them uniform, about the size of a walnut or 1-inch in diameter.

In a large skillet, heat remaining olive oil over medium heat. Dredge, or roll the meatballs in flour. Tap to remove excess flour. Fry them in small batches in the skillet, about 3 minutes on each side. They should be golden brown on the outside and no longer pink on the inside.

Remove from the pan and place on paper towels to drain the excess fat. Place on platter and garnish with lemon wedges, or serve with Tiganites Patates as a meal.

WorldwideGreeks.com **favorite**

Saganaki
Pan Seared Cheese

mezze

SERVES 4

INGREDIENTS

1 cup all-purpose flour

¼ teaspoon salt

¼ cup olive oil

8 ounces Kasseri or Gruyere cheese

1 cup cold water

Lemon wedges

INSTRUCTIONS

Whisk the flour and salt together in a large mixing bowl. Set aside.

Add the olive oil to a small, heavy skillet and heat over medium-high heat.

Cut the cheese ½ inch thick and 3 inches wide and then place it into the bowl along with the flour. Toss it gently with a wooden spoon to coat the cheese cubes with flour on all side. Dip each piece in the water.

Repeat that process two more times. Place it into the pan and fry each side for about 2-3 minutes or until golden.

Remove from the heat and set aside. Serve hot with a squeeze of lemon juice.

WorldwideGreeks.com **favorite**

Garides Saganaki
Shrimp Saganaki

mezze

SERVES 6-8

INGREDIENTS

1 pound shrimp, u-15 size or smaller

3 tablespoons olive oil

1 onion, finely chopped

3 garlic cloves, minced

1 teaspoon ground fennel

2 tablespoons fresh parsley, chopped

Pinch of chili flakes (or more to taste)

1 tablespoon tomato paste

1½ cups finely diced tomatoes

¼ cup plus 1 tablespoon ouzo, divided

Juice of half a lemon

¾ teaspoon salt

Pinch of sugar

⅓ cup freshly crumbled feta cheese

Freshly ground black pepper

Bread, for serving

INSTRUCTIONS

Peel and devein the shrimp, set aside in a bowl.

In a large ovenproof skillet, heat the oil over medium-high heat. Add the onions and sauté, about 5-6 minutes. Add the garlic, ground fennel seed, half of the parsley, chili flakes, tomato paste and stir to combine. Sauté for 2 minutes. Stir in the tomatoes, ¼ cup ouzo, lemon, salt, sugar and reduce until almost all the liquid has evaporated, about 10 minutes.

While the mixture is sautéing, preheat the broiler on high heat.

Add the shrimp to the tomato sauce, ⅔ of the feta, 1 tablespoon of ouzo and the remaining parsley. Season the sauce with freshly ground black pepper. Mix quickly and bring back to a simmer. Cook until the shrimp turn pink and are done.

Remove the pan from heat. Sprinkle the remaining feta over the top. Place under the broiler for 1-2 minutes. Serve immediately with plenty of crusty bread for dipping or as part of a meal. Serve with Pilafi and a Horiatikito make it a meal.

Kolokythokeftedes
Zucchini Fritters

mezze

SERVES 6-8

INGREDIENTS

1 pound zucchini

½ teaspoon salt

½ onion, grated

1-2 scallions, chopped (white and green parts)

1 garlic clove, smashed and finely minced

2 tablespoons fresh dill, finely chopped

1 tablespoon fresh mint, finely chopped

2 eggs, beaten

¾ cup feta cheese

¼ cup shredded Kefalotiri, Gruyere, or Parmesan cheese

½ cup breadcrumbs

¼ cup self-rising flour

Freshly ground pepper

Olive or vegetable oil, for frying

¾ cup flour

Salt and pepper, to taste

INSTRUCTIONS

Coarsely grate the zucchini either by hand (box grater using the large holes) or in a food processor fitted with a coarse grating disk.

In a fine-mesh strainer, place the zucchini and sprinkle with the salt.

Mix thoroughly, and let it drain in the sink for 15 minutes. Squeeze out as much liquid as possible. Squeeze again after preparing the rest of the ingredient to ensure the majority of water is gone. The drier the zucchini, the crispier the fritters will become.

Meanwhile, in a large bowl, add the onion, scallions, garlic, dill, mint, eggs, feta cheese, kefalotiri, breadcrumbs, self rising flour and freshly ground pepper. Using your hands, mix until the mixture is just firm enough to turn into small patties. Do not over mix. Add a little more breadcrumbs if the mixture is too wet.

Form the zucchini mixture into 2-inch balls. Lightly push the balls down to form into patties.

Cover the bottom of a large saucepan with ½ inch of oil and set it over medium-high heat.

Coat each zucchini patty in the flour, shaking to remove any excess. Carefully place them into the oil. Do not overcrowd your pan, to ensure you can easily flip them. Cook in batches if necessary. Fry both sides of the zucchini fritter until nice and golden brown.

Remove fritters from the oil and drain on a large plate lined with paper towel. Serve the Kolokythokeftedes hot or cold with a side of Tzatziki.

Notes: You can line the strainer with a cheesecloth or tea towel. Gather, twist and squeeze the towel to remove excess liquid.

Skordalia
Garlic Potato Dip

mezze

SERVES 8-10

INGREDIENTS

1½ pounds Yukon Gold potatoes

1½ teaspoons salt

½ cup extra virgin olive oil

½ teaspoon salt

4 tablespoons red wine vinegar

5 garlic cloves, green parts removed

Freshly ground white or black pepper

Toasted baguette slices, chopped parsley for serving

INSTRUCTIONS

Peel the potatoes and cut them into 2-inch pieces.

In a large pot, add water and 1 teaspoon salt. Bring to a rolling boil and add the potatoes. Reduce heat to medium and simmer until tender, about 15 - 20 minutes. The boiling time depends on how thick you cut your potato pieces. Reserve ¼ cup of cooking water.

Drain the potatoes thoroughly and place them in a large bowl. Meanwhile, in a food processor fitted with the steel blade or in the jar of a blender, process the extra virgin olive oil, ½ teaspoon salt, vinegar and garlic until nice and smooth.

Mash the potatoes using a potato masher, adding the garlic oil mixture in about 3 parts. Mash as you go along, until the potatoes are creamy and well combined but still hold a bit of texture. Taste and adjust the seasoning, and vinegar if necessary.

The mixture should look like loose mashed potatoes. If the consistency is too thick, add 1 tablespoon of reserved potato water or a little olive oil to loosen the Skordalia up.

Cover with plastic wrap and refrigerate for at least 3 hours before serving. Drizzle with some extra virgin olive oil and chopped parsley.

Serve as part of a larger platter or with Grilled Branzino and Horta to make it a meal.

Notes: The intensity of the garlic will increase over time so it is important to give a chance for the flavors to develop. Do not use a food processor to mash the potatoes. It changes the texture of the dip and makes the potatoes feel gummy.

WorldwideGreeks.com **favorite**

salads & soups

ΡΙΓΑΝΗ
1.€
ΡΙΓΑΝΗ
5 €
ΡΙΓΑΝΗ
1.€
ΛΟΥΙΖΑ
1.€
ΤΣΑΙ ΒΟΥΝΟΥ

The Herbs of
Greek Cuisine

Greek cuisine takes advantage of the abundance of herbs growing throughout the country. Fresh or dried, these herbs create a robust flavor profile which is incorporated in many of the traditional dishes. Some of the most common herbs include:

OREGANO
There is no herb used more frequently in Greek cuisine than oregano. You will have a hard time finding a popular Greek dish that does not feature this frangrant herb. Greek oregano is popular because of its great taste and versatility, and is used to flavor salads, soups, and meat marinades.

THYME
Thyme has a similar flavor profile to oregano, as the plants are in the same family. To those unfamiliar with the herbs, it is sometimes difficult to distinguish the two. The thyme plant has smaller leaves and the flavor is milder than oregano. Thyme is very common in Greek cuisine and can stand on its own, or as a replacement for oregano. Most commonly, thyme is typically paired with chicken in Greek cooking.

PARSLEY
Parsley is generally thought of as a garnish in many cultures, but in Greek cuisine it is a crucial ingredient in many dishes. Parsley has a very delicate flavor, and should only be used fresh when added to dishes. Unlike other popular herbs, parsley's flavor completely disappears when dried. There are two common types of parsley, curly and flat leaf. Flat leaf parsley has a stronger scent and flavor and is typically used in Greek cooking.

MINT
Mint is a polarizing herb due to its very strong flavor, but it is absolutely adored by the Greeks. While most countries reserve mint for flavoring drinks and desserts, the Greeks love putting this potent herb in their savory dishes. Mint pairs extremely well with ground lamb and spinach, so it is most commonly used in Greek meatballs and Spanakopita.

BAY LEAVES
The bay palm tree can be found growing all over Greece. This tree is best known for producing delicious bay leaves. Since they are so abundant in the country, bay leaves are regularly used in Greek cooking. Bay leaves need to be cooked a long time to coax out their wonderful flavor. This is why they are mostly used in stews and soups. Bay leaves also work well as a seasoning on braised meats.

DILL
Pickling vegetables is a common tradition in Greece because it is a great way to preserve the leftover crops before they go bad. Dill is the main herb using during the pickling process to add flavor to the vegetables. You will also likely find fresh dill finely chopped and sprinkled on the top of many Greek salads.

Horiatiki Salata
Village Salad

salad

SERVES 4-6

INGREDIENTS

4-5 large, vine ripened tomatoes

1 cucumber, peeled and sliced

1 small white onion, thinly sliced

⅓ cup extra virgin olive oil

1 ½ teaspoons dried oregano

Salt and freshly ground black pepper, to taste

7 ounces feta cheese, drained and cut into thick slabs

8 Kalamata olives

INSTRUCTIONS

Cut the tomatoes in bite size wedges over a serving bowl to catch the tomato juices. Peel your cucumber and cut lengthwise.

Slice the cucumber into ¼" pieces and add them to the serving bowl. Add onion and drizzle the olive oil over the salad.

Crush the oregano with your fingers in order to release its wonderful fragrant aroma. Season with salt and pepper. Toss the salad for a few minutes, and set it aside. Just before serving, place the feta and olives on top.

Drizzle some extra virgin olive oil over the feta and sprinkle with more oregano. Serve with fresh bread or accompanying any meal.

Notes: The most sought-after part of the Horiatiki amongst Greeks is the juice that sits at the bottom of the bowl. Rip pieces of the bread and soak them in the juice as a flavorful addition to your meal.

WorldwideGreeks.com **favorite**

Lahanosalata
Cabbage Salad

salad

SERVES 4-6

INGREDIENTS

1 small white cabbage, shredded

2-3 carrots, shredded

½ cup extra virgin olive oil

5 tablespoons fresh lemon juice

⅛ teaspoon dried garlic powder

½ teaspoon salt

INSTRUCTIONS

In a large bowl, toss together the cabbage and carrots. Place the olive oil, lemon juice, garlic granules and salt in a small bowl and whisk with a fork until homogenized.

Add the dressing on top of the salad and toss. Taste and adjust the seasoning, if necessary.

Serve as a side with Biftekia me Patates or grilled meats.

Notes: The amount of olive oil and lemon juice depends on your own tastes. The amounts listed above are a guideline. Start out with half the stated amount, if desired, and add more to taste. Feel free to substitute white cabbage for red, or use ½ a white cabbage and ½ a red cabbage. The flavors are similar, but the red cabbage gives it some color.

Pantzaria me Skordalia
Roasted Beets with Garlic Potato Dip

salad

SERVES 4-6

INGREDIENTS

4 medium red beets, washed

2 tablespoons extra virgin olive oil

Salt and freshly ground black pepper, to taste

1 cup water

Extra-virgin olive oil for drizzling

1 tablespoon red or white wine vinegar

1 recipe Skordalia Page 35

Thinly sliced scallions, to garnish

INSTRUCTIONS

Preheat the oven to 425°F.

If the beets have the greens attached, cut them off, within ½ inch of the beets. Reserve the greens for another use. Don't pierce the beets. In a small square baking dish, add the beets and drizzle with 2 tablespoons olive oil.

Season with salt and pepper and pour in the water. Cover pan tightly with foil and crimp edges to form a seal.

Bake beets until a knife pierces the beets easily, about 1 hour. Transfer the pan to a rack and carefully uncover. Once they are cool enough to handle, peel the beets and cut into 1"–2" pieces. Place them in a bowl and allow to them cool.

Drizzle with extra virgin olive oil and 1 tablespoon wine vinegar and toss gently. Spoon the Skordalia onto a serving platter, spreading it thinly. Top with the beets, season with salt and pepper and scatter the scallions on top.

Notes: The beets can be prepared up to 1 day ahead. If you do that, you will want to cover the bowl with plastic wrap and refrigerate. Warm it up it slightly before serving.

Kota Avgolemono
Chicken Soup

soup

SERVES 6-8

INGREDIENTS

- 1 large, free-range chicken
- 8 cups homemade or store-bought chicken stock, divided
- 1 large onion, finely chopped
- 2 carrots, sliced
- 2 celery stalks, chopped
- Salt, freshly ground pepper
- 1 cup dried white rice
- 2 large eggs
- 2 lemons

INSTRUCTIONS

In a 5-quart or larger Dutch oven, add the chicken, stock, onion, carrots, celery and salt. Cover and bring to a boil. Reduce heat to medium-low and simmer until the chicken is cooked through, about 50 minutes - 1 hour.

Using a slotted spoon, skim off and discard any white foam that rises to the top. Remove the chicken from the pot and set aside. With a large spoon, skim off any fat rendered from the chicken. Stir in the rice and simmer uncovered, until tender, about 15-20 minutes.

Meanwhile remove the chicken meat from the bones and shred the meat into bite sized pieces, set aside. Discard the skin and bones.

Return the reserved shredded chicken to the pot, and reduce to low heat. In a medium bowl, whisk the eggs until frothy and lightened in color, about 2 minutes.

Gradually whisk in the lemon juice until combined. Temper in the eggs by slowly adding a ladle full of warm stock into the egg-lemon mixture, whisking continuously. This warms the eggs just enough so that they do not curdle when added to the hot soup.

Slowly stir the egg-lemon mixture back into the soup. Whisk quickly so as not to scramble the eggs. Cook until the soup thickens slightly, 3 to 4 minutes, but do not let it come to a boil. Taste and adjust the seasoning, if necessary.

Place the soup into serving bowls and serve with plenty of lemon slices. Serve immediately.

Notes: Leftovers can be stored in an airtight container in the refrigerator for up to 2 days. Reheat on the stove over low heat, making sure not to boil the soup. The chicken and stock can be prepared 2 days in advance. Shred the chicken and refrigerate separately. Strain the stock and refrigerate. The lemon can be juiced ahead of time as well.

WorldwideGreeks.com **favorite**

Fakes
Lentil Soup

soup

SERVES 4-6

INGREDIENTS

1 pound dried brown lentils

2 tablespoons olive oil

1 onion, diced

2 cloves garlic, finely chopped

¼ cup canned tomato puree

4 cups vegetable stock

2 bay leaves

¼ cup extra virgin olive oil

1 ½ teaspoons salt

Pepper, to taste

Red wine vinegar (optional, for serving)

INSTRUCTIONS

In a fine mesh colander, rinse the lentils under cold running water. Place the lentils in a large pot with just enough water to cover them, and bring to a boil. Cook for 5 minutes, then drain.

In the same pot, heat 2 tablespoon of the olive oil over medium heat. Add the onion, garlic and sauté until both have softened. Stir in the lentils, tomato puree, stock, and bay leaves. Bring soup to a boil.

Reduce heat to medium-low, cover and simmer for 50-60 minutes or until the lentils are tender. When the soup is ready, add the olive oil in a slow steady stream and stir until the soup slightly thickens, about 5 minutes.

Discard the bay leaves and stir in the salt and pepper.

Transfer the lentil soup to serving bowls and add 1 tablespoon of vinegar to each (optional). Serve with toasted bread and olives on the side.

Notes: Feel free to add a stalk or two of chopped carrots and/or celery to your soup. Let them sauté with onions.

Fasolada
Bean Soup

soup

SERVES 4-6

INGREDIENTS

1 pound dried beans (gigantes, butter, lima, or navy beans)

1 teaspoon salt

8 cups vegetable stock

3 carrots, cut into cubes

2 onions, finely chopped

3 celery stalks with their green leaves, finely chopped

2 cloves garlic

2 tablespoon tomato paste

¾ cup olive oil

Salt and pepper to taste

1 teaspoon bukovo or red pepper, optional

INSTRUCTIONS

In a large bowl, add the beans and cover with cold water by about 3 inches. Add 1 teaspoon of salt and gently stir. Allow them to soak for about 8-12 hours (or overnight).

Strain the beans and put into a large soup pot or Dutch oven. Add enough water to cover the beans completely and bring to a gentle boil.

Reduce the heat to medium. Cook for about 5 minutes. Transfer the beans to a colander and drain.

In the same pot, add the vegetable stock, beans, carrots, onions, celery, garlic, tomato paste. Bring the soup to a boil. Cover the pot and turn the heat to medium-low. Simmer the soup for about 1 hour.

Add more water if necessary. Add the olive oil, salt and pepper and continue cooking for 15–20 minutes more, until the soup is thick and creamy, and the beans and vegetables are tender. Serve with fresh bread, feta cheese and olives.

WorldwideGreeks.com **favorite**

Hortosoupa
Vegetable Soup

soup

SERVES 4-6

INGREDIENTS

3 tablespoons olive oil

1 medium white onion, diced

2 carrots, diced

2 celery stalks, diced

1 leek, white and light green part, finely chopped

8 ounces mushrooms, diced

1 small zucchini, diced

1 garlic, minced

1 teaspoon chopped fresh thyme

8 cups low sodium vegetable stock (or chicken stock)

2 medium potatoes, diced

1 small tomato, grated

½ teaspoon salt

¼ teaspoon freshly ground pepper

⅔ cups orzo

½ juice of a lemon (or more to taste)

3 tablespoons chopped fresh parsley

INSTRUCTIONS

In a large stockpot, heat the olive oil over medium-high heat. Add the onion, carrots, celery, leeks, mushrooms, zucchini, garlic, thyme, and cook stirring occasionally until the vegetables begin to soften, about 5 minutes.

Add the stock, potatoes, tomatoes with whatever juices have accumulated, salt and pepper, and bring to a boil. Reduce the heat to low and bring to a slow simmer. Cover and simmer for about 20 minutes.

Add the orzo and cook for 10-15 minutes more until the vegetables are fork tender. Remove from the heat and add the lemon juice and parsley. Taste and adjust the seasoning, if necessary. Serve immediately.

Soupa me Domata kai Kritharaki
Tomato soup with Orzo

soup

SERVES 4-6

INGREDIENTS

3 tomatoes grated or 1 (28-ounce) can crushed tomatoes,

3 tablespoons olive oil

2 medium yellow onions, chopped

1 clove garlic, minced

1 tablespoon tomato paste

1 shot of ouzo (about ¼ cup) or white wine

5 ½ cups chicken stock,

Salt and freshly ground black pepper

⅔ cup orzo

Pinch of Boukovo (optional) or smoky chili pepper

GRILLED FETA CHEESE CROUTONS:

4 (½-inch-thick) slices country white bread

2 tablespoons unsalted butter, melted

2 ounces mozzarella cheese, shredded

4 ounces feta cheese, crumbled

INSTRUCTIONS

Coarsely grate the tomatoes with box grater using the large holes. Squeeze the grated tomato with your hands to remove most of its juice. Strain the juice into a small bowl and set aside.

In a large pot or Dutch oven, heat the olive oil over medium heat. Add the onions and sauté until translucent, about 10 minutes. Add the garlic and sauté for 1 more minute. Add the grated tomatoes, tomato paste and sauté for 2 minutes. Deglaze with the pan with the shot of ouzo. Stir in the chicken stock, juice from the tomatoes, ½ tablespoon salt and ½ teaspoon pepper. Increase the heat to medium high and bring to a boil. Cover and reduce heat to medium low.

Simmer for 15 minutes. Add the orzo pasta, cover the pot and simmer for an additional 15 minutes, occasionally stirring. Serve hot with a pinch of boukovo and Grilled Feta Cheese Croutons scattered on top.

Grilled Feta Cheese Croutons

Heat a small non-stick skillet over medium-high heat.

Place the four slices of bread on a cutting board and brush lightly with the melted butter. Turn the slices over and spread Mozzarella and Feta cheese evenly over two slices of bread. Place the remaining two slices of bread on top of the Mozzarella and Feta cheese.

Butter the top slices of bread as well. Grill the sandwiches about 4 minutes per side or until nicely browned. Place on a cutting board and allow to rest for 1 minute and cut into 1-inch cubes.

WorldwideGreeks.com **favorite**

pita

The Wild Greens
of Greece

The hills and mountains of Greece are rich with herbs, teas and greens that locals have been foraging since ancient times. There are many self-sufficient villages and islands where people walk the lands and pick what they need. Wild greens, or Horta, are plentiful and integrated into many Greek recipes. Horta, in any combination, can be used in dishes such as Hortopita, Spanakorizo or Prasopita. It is also common to serve simply prepared Horta, with a drizzle of olive oil, squeeze of lemon and a pinch of salt, as a side dish. Some common wild greens readily found in Greece include:

DANDELION
Dandelion greens, known as radikia, grow wild in many countries. Dandelions can be invasive and therefore many people treat them as weeds, rather than ingredients. These nutrient dense greens are packed with vitamins K, C and A and are a great source of minerals. If you are lucky to live in an area where dandelions grow wild, grab some scissors and a basket and forage. When cooking wild dandelion greens, it is helpful to bring them to a boil with fresh water 2-3 times to help balance any bitterness.

LAMB'S QUARTERS
Lamb's Quarters, or Levethies are used in salads and also incorporated into pitas such as hortopita. They are high in protein and fiber, and loaded with vitamins A and C. Lamb's quarters are also a source of Omega-3 and Omega-6 fatty acids.

AMARANTH
Amaranth greens, or vleeta, contain seeds that centuries ago, were used as a type of grain. Amaranth seeds can be ground down into a powder and turned into a gluten-free bread. Vleeta are a great antioxidant and are known to reduce inflammation and lower cholesterol levels. These greens are commonly eaten boiled and drizzled with olive oil and lemon. They can also be incorporated into Hortopita.

NETTLE
Nettle, or tsouknides is a stubborn plant that contains stingers. Picking tsouknides is not an easy task, but worth the effort. This green is high in antioxidants and vitamin C and in ancient times was used to treat arthritis and muscle pain. Once cooked, the stingers die off and what's left is a delicious, succulent green that has a distinct, and delicious, flavor. You can also dry the leaves of this plant and make a nourishing tea.

Tiropita
Cheese Pie

pita

MAKES 12 LARGE OR 24 SMALL PIECES

INGREDIENTS

4 eggs

¼ cup milk

1 ¼ pounds feta cheese, crumbled

9 ounces fresh anthotyro or cottage cheese

Freshly ground pepper

¼ teaspoon nutmeg

ASSEMBLY:

⅔ cup butter, melted or ½ cup olive oil

Box of phyllo dough, thawed and at room temperature. 9"x13", approximately 18-20 sheets.

Water, to sprinkle on top

White or black sesame seeds (optional)

INSTRUCTIONS

Preheat the oven to 400°F. Lightly brush a 9x13 ovenproof dish or baking pan with butter. Arrange the rack in the middle of the oven.

In a large bowl, lightly beat the eggs. Whisk in the milk, feta cheese, anthotyro cheese, pepper and nutmeg. Set aside.

Carefully unroll the phyllo sheets and lay them flat. Cover with a damp cloth to prevent them from drying out. Place 1 phyllo sheet off-center in the pan and let the edges hang over the sides. Brush the top sheet with butter taking care not to brush over the hanging sides. Place another phyllo on the other side, letting the edges hang over the sides. Brush the top sheet with butter taking care not to brush over the hanging sides. Continue on with this process until you have used half of the phyllo sheets.

Pour the filling into the pan and smooth out evenly using an offset spatula. Fold the overhanging phyllo over the filling.

Continue to layer the remaining phyllo sheets over the filling. Trim the overhang and with a pastry brush, push the edges into the sides so they disappear. Using a knife, score into 12 or 24 even pieces. Be careful not to cut all the way through. Brush the top with butter and sprinkle with a little water.

Bake until golden brown, which should take about 1 hour. Let it cool for at least 45 minutes. Cut into squares and serve.

The cheese pie can be enjoyed warm or cold and can be stored in the refrigerator up to a week

Notes: The pie can be assembled, wrapped well and frozen for up to 1 month. It can be baked straight from the freezer. Increase oven time to about 1 ½ hours when baking straight from the freezer. To crisp up refrigerated leftovers, reheat in a 300°F oven for 15 to 20 minutes.

WorldwideGreeks.com **favorite**

Spanakopita
Spinach Pie

pita

MAKES 12 LARGE
OR 24 SMALL PIECES

INGREDIENTS

2 bags spinach, washed and roughly chopped (2 pounds)

1 onion, grated

4 spring onions, finely chopped (optional)

2 tablespoons fresh dill, chopped (optional)

8 oz feta cheese, crumbled

¼ cup olive oil

2 large eggs, beaten

Salt and pepper, to taste

ASSEMBLY:

⅔ cup butter, melted or ½ cup olive oil

Box of phyllo dough, thawed and at room temperature. 9"x13", approximately 18-20 sheets

Water, to sprinkle on top

INSTRUCTIONS

Finely chop the spinach and place in a large colander. Sprinkle evenly with salt. Massage the spinach until it wilts. Place a heavy weight on top of the spinach (a large dinner plate topped with a few cans works well) and leave for 1 hour to drain.

Preheat the oven to 400°F. Lightly brush a 9x13 ovenproof dish or baking pan with butter. Arrange the rack in the middle of the oven.

Squeeze the spinach in handfuls until no more liquid comes out (it should look thoroughly wilted and dry). Place in a large bowl, add onion, spring onion, dill, feta cheese, olive oil and eggs and mix well. Season with salt and pepper, remembering that feta is salty and the spinach has been salted. Unroll the phyllo sheets and lay them flat. Cover with a damp cloth to prevent them from drying out.

Place 1 phyllo sheet off-center in the pan and let the edges hang over the sides. Brush the top sheet with butter taking care not to brush over the hanging sides. Place another phyllo sheet on the other side, letting the edges hang over the sides. Brush the top sheet with butter taking care not to brush over the hanging sides. Continue on with this process until you have used half of the phyllo sheets.

Pour the filling into the pan and smooth out evenly using an offset spatula. Fold the overhanging phyllo over the filling. Continue to layer the remaining phyllo sheets over the filling. Trim the overhang and with a pastry brush push the edges into the sides so they disappear.

Using a knife, score into 12 or 24 even pieces. Be careful not to cut all the way through. Brush the top with butter and sprinkle with a little water.

Bake for about 1 hour or until the phyllo is golden brown. Let the pie cool for at least 30 minutes before serving. Serve warm, at room temperature or chilled.

Variation: Hortopita - Wild Greens Pie
To make Hortopita, follow the steps above for Spanakopita with one addition. Mix the spinach with other wild herbs of your choice such as: dandelion greens, fennel, kale, and amaranth.

WorldwideGreeks.com **favorite**

Kolokythopita
Zucchini Pie

pita

MAKES 12 LARGE OR 24 SMALL PIECES

INGREDIENTS

2 pounds zucchini, grated, squeezed and drained

4 spring onions, cut into thin slices

1 large onion grated

½ bunch dill, finely chopped

½ bunch parsley, finely chopped

¼ cup olive oil

2 eggs lightly beaten

12 ounces. feta, crushed

3 ½ ounces Gruyere, coarsely grated

7 ounces cottage cheese

3 tablespoons fine semolina

3 tablespoons all-purpose flour

Salt and freshly ground pepper, to taste

ASSEMBLY:

⅔ cup butter, melted or ½ cup olive oil

Box of phyllo dough, thawed and at room temperature. 9"x13", approximately 18-20 sheets.

Water to sprinkle on top

INSTRUCTIONS

Place the grated zucchini in a colander and set it in the sink. Using your hands, squeeze the grated zucchini to extract as much water as possible. Generously sprinkle salt over the zucchini and toss; Set aside.

Preheat the oven to 400°F. Lightly brush a 9x13 ovenproof dish or baking pan with olive oil. Arrange the rack in the middle of the oven.

In a large bowl, combine the grated onion, dill, parsley, olive oil, eggs, feta cheese, Gruyere, cottage cheese and a good pinch of pepper. Squeeze the zucchini a couple more times to extract more water, then fold the zucchini, flour and semolina into the cheese mixture. Unroll the phyllo sheets and lay them flat. Cover with a damp cloth to prevent them from drying out. Place 1 phyllo sheet off-center in the pan and let the edges hang over the sides. Brush the top sheet with butter taking care not to brush over the hanging sides. Place another phyllo sheet on the other side, letting the edges hang over the sides. Brush the top sheet with butter taking care not to brush over the hanging sides. Continue on with this process until you have used half of the phyllo sheets.

Pour the filling into the pan and smooth out evenly using an offset spatula. Fold the overhanging phyllo over the filling. Continue to layer the remaining phyllo sheets over the filling. Trim the overhang and with a pastry brush, push the edges into the sides so they disappear.

Using a knife, score into 12 or 24 even pieces. Be careful not to cut all the way through. Brush the top with any remaining butter and sprinkle with a little water. Sprinkle the surface of the phyllo with a little water.

Bake for about 1 hour or until the phyllo is golden brown. Let the pie cool for at least 30 minutes before serving. Serve warm, at room temperature or chilled.

Notes: The pie can be assembled, wrapped well and frozen for up to 1 month. It can be baked straight from the freezer. Increase oven time to about 1 ½ hours when baking straight from the freezer. To crisp up refrigerated leftovers, reheat in a 300°F oven for 15 to 20 minutes.

Prassopita
Leek Pie

pita

**MAKES 12 LARGE
OR 24 SMALL PIECES**

INGREDIENTS

5-6 tablespoons olive oil

2 pounds leeks, halved lengthwise, washed, dried, and thinly sliced

2 spring onions, thinly sliced

1 small onion

2 large eggs

3 tablespoons semolina

⅓ dill bunch, finely chopped

1 teaspoon fresh mint,finely chopped

10 ounces feta cheese crumbled

1 teaspoon salt

½ teaspoon pepper

ASSEMBLY:

⅔ cup butter, melted or ½ cup extra virgin olive oil

Box of phyllo dough, thawed and at room temperature. 9"x13", approximately 18-20 sheets.

Water, to sprinkle on top

INSTRUCTIONS

Preheat the oven to 400°F. Lightly brush a 9x13 ovenproof dish or baking pan with oil. Arrange the rack in the middle of the oven.

In a large sauté pan, heat the olive oil over medium-high heat and sauté the leeks, about 5 minutes. Add spring onions, onion and sauté, about 3-4 minutes. In a medium bowl, lightly beat the eggs. Add the cooked leeks and onions mixture, semolina, dill, mint, salt, pepper and feta cheese. Toss to combine and set aside.

In a small pot, heat the butter over medium heat until melted. Unroll the phyllo sheets and lay them flat. Covered with a damp cloth to prevent them from drying out.

Place 1 phyllo dough off-center in the pan and let the edges hang over the sides. Brush the top sheet with butter taking care not to brush over the hanging sides. Place another phyllo on the other side, letting the edges hang over the sides. Brush the top sheet with butter taking care not to brush over the hanging sides. Continue on with this process until you have used half of the phyllo sheets.

Pour the filling into the pan and smooth out evenly using an offset spatula. Fold the overhanging phyllo over the filling. Continue to layer the remaining phyllo sheets over the filling. Trim the overhang and with a pastry brush push the edges into the sides so they disappear.

Using a knife, score into 12 or 24 even pieces. Be careful not to cut all the way through. Brush the top with any remaining butter and sprinkle with a little water.

Bake for 1 hour, or until golden brown. Let cool until just warm. Serve the pieces carefully, cutting out the rectangles carefully along the score marks and serve.

Tips: For a variation, try making individual Prasopita into triangles.
For instructions on how to do this, visit the food forum on WorldwideGreeks.com

Notes: The pie can be assembled, wrapped well and frozen for up to 1 month. It can be baked straight from the freezer. Increase oven time to about 1 ½ hours when baking straight from the freezer. To crisp up refrigerated leftovers, reheat in a 300°F oven for 15 to 20 minutes.

Kreatopita
Meat Pie

pita

**MAKES 12 LARGE
OR 24 SMALL PIECES**

INGREDIENTS

¼ cup olive oil

4 leeks, washed and thinly sliced (white part only)

1 large onion, finely diced

1 ½ pound ground beef (or a mix of beef, pork or lamb)

1 teaspoon oregano

½ bunch fresh parsley, finely chopped

½ teaspoon tomato paste

1 vegetable bouillon cube

Salt and pepper, to taste

⅓ cup white wine

¼ cup water

⅔ cups kasseri or Gruyere cheese

1 large egg, lightly beaten

For the assembly:

⅔ cup butter, melted or ½ cup extra virgin olive oil

Box of phyllo dough, thawed and at room temperature. 9"x13", approximately 18-20 sheets.

Water, to sprinkle on top

INSTRUCTIONS

Preheat the oven to 400°F. Lightly brush a 9x13 ovenproof dish or baking pan with butter. Arrange the rack in the middle of the oven.

In a large sauté pan, heat the olive oil over medium-high heat. Add the leeks, onion and sauté for about 5 minutes. Add the ground beef and break it up with a wooden spoon. Sauté for 3-4 minutes, until it browns nicely.

Once the meat is brown, add the oregano, parsley, tomato paste, vegetable cube, salt and pepper. Stir to combine. Add the wine and water stirring after each addition. Once all liquid has been reduced, remove from heat and empty into the bowl. Let it cool for 5 minutes.

Add the cheese and egg and mix to combine. Set meat mixture aside. Unroll the phyllo sheets and lay them flat. Covered with a damp cloth to prevent them from drying out.

Place 1 phyllo dough off-center in the pan and let the edges hang over the sides. Brush the top sheet with butter taking care not to brush over the hanging sides. Place another phyllo on the other side, letting the edges hang over the sides. Brush the top sheet with butter taking care not to brush over the hanging sides. Continue on with this process until you have used half of the phyllo sheets. Pour the meat mixture into the pan and smooth out evenly. Fold the overhanging phyllo over the filling.

Continue to layer the remaining phyllo sheets over the meat mixture. Trim the overhang and with a brush push the edges into the sides so they disappear. Drizzle the remaining butter over the top.

Using a knife, score into 12 even pieces. Be careful not to cut all the way through. Brush the top with any remaining butter and sprinkle with a little water. Bake for 1 hour and 10 minutes or until golden brown and flaky. Let it cool, slice and serve!

Notes: The pie can be assembled, wrapped well and frozen for up to 1 month. It can be baked straight from the freezer. Increase oven time to about 1 ½ hours when baking straight from the freezer. To crisp up refrigerated leftovers, reheat in a 300°F oven for 15 to 20 minutes.

WorldwideGreeks.com **favorite**

main plates

What is Greek Feta Cheese?

Greek feta is a type of cheese made from sheep's or goat's milk, which has been described as tasting "tangy, salty, and rich." It is made in Greece and has played an integral role in Greek cuisine since ancient times. Today it is enjoyed around the world for its savory salty flavor. In Greece, feta is typically sold as a small 1 pound (500g) block. Feta is a staple in Greece households and is typically served as an accompaniment to most meals.

History of Greek Feta cheese

Feta is indigenous to Greece, where the most popular variety is called "salty" cheese. It dates back to the Minoan era and has been made in families for generations. Feta cheese was traditionally made from either 100% sheep's milk or a blend of sheep's and goat's milk during winter as a way to store extra milk. However, nowadays, it can be produced year-round due to factory production methods.

Protection of its geographical origin (PDO) was granted to Greek feta cheese in 2002. Therefore, only feta produced in Greece can claim to be authentic. While feta is made in other regions (such as Israel and France), PDO standards state that these cheese versions must be renamed or labeled as "feta-style" to avoid confusion.

Moussaka
Eggplant and Ground Beef Pie

main plate

MAKES 9 PIECES

INGREDIENTS

VEGETABLES:

3 large eggplants

3 large potatoes peeled and thinly sliced

MEAT SAUCE:

⅓ cup olive oil

1 large onion, chopped

1 garlic clove

1 ½ pounds ground beef

2 fresh tomatoes, grated

½ cup canned tomato puree

1 teaspoon sugar

¼ teaspoon cinnamon

Generous pinch ground clove

2 tablespoons parsley

Salt and pepper to taste

⅓ cup veggie stock or water

Olive oil for frying

BECHAMEL SAUCE:

¾ cup unsalted butter

¾ cup all purpose flour

6 cups milk

Generous pinch nutmeg

2 yolks, beaten

⅔ cups kefalograviera cheese, (or Gruyere) grated

Salt & pepper to taste

INSTRUCTIONS

Sprinkle the eggplants with salt and place them in a colander. Set aside for 30 minutes to drain their water.

Meanwhile, in a medium pot, heat the oil over medium-high heat. Add the chopped onions and sauté, about 4-5 minutes. Add the garlic sauté for a minute. Add the beef, breaking it up with a wooden spoon. Cook until the mixture is almost dry. Add the grated tomato, tomato puree and sauté for 2-3 minutes.

Add the sugar, cinnamon, cloves, parsley and season with salt and pepper. Add the stock and bring to a boil. Cover and reduce the heat to medium-low and simmer for 25-30 minutes, until the sauce thickens and the juices evaporate. Meanwhile, rinse the eggplants and pat dry with a kitchen paper. In a frying pan add plenty of olive oil, and fry the eggplants on both sides until nicely golden brown. Place the eggplants on a plate layered with kitchen paper. Add more oil to the pan if needed. Fry the potato slices and place on kitchen paper as well.

For the Béchamel Sauce: Melt the butter in a deep saucepan over a medium heat. Add the flour in stages, continuously whisking until the mixture is smooth. Whisk in the milk and continue whisking until thickened and creamy, about 12 to 15 minutes. Remove sauce pan from the heat and whisk in the nutmeg. Let the sauce cool for a minute or two. Whisk in 2 lightly beaten egg yolks. Add ⅔ of the cheese and stir till incorporated. Season to taste. Preheat oven to 400°F.

Brush 9x13 baking dish with olive oil. Arrange potatoes in an overlapping layer and sprinkle with kefalograviera cheese. Add an overlapping layer of eggplants and sprinkle with cheese. Add 2-3 tablespoons of béchamel sauce to the beef mixture and mix. Spread the ground meat over the vegetables. Pour the béchamel sauce over the beef, covering entire surface of dish. Sprinkle with remaining cheese on top.

Place the dish in the oven and bake for 50-60 minutes. The Moussaka should be bubbly, golden on top, and slightly browned around the edges. Remove it from the oven and let it rest for at least 30- 40minutes before serving.

Notes: For a lighter version of the traditional Moussaka, brush the eggplant and potatoes with oil and salt and bake in a preheated oven at 400°F until soft.

Pastitsio
Macaroni Pie

main plate

SERVES 4-6

INGREDIENTS

MEAT SAUCE:

- ⅓ cup olive oil
- 1 large onion, finely chopped
- 1 garlic clove
- 1 pound ground beef
- 2 fresh tomatoes, grated
- 1 tablespoon tomato paste
- 1 teaspoon sugar
- ¼ teaspoon cinnamon
- ¼ teaspoon allspice
- Salt and pepper, to taste
- ½ cup veggie stock or water
- 2 tablespoons parsley

PASTA:

- 8 ounces bucatini pasta
- 1 cup of kefalograviera grated cheese

BECHAMEL SAUCE:

- ¾ cup unsalted butter
- ¾ cup all-purpose flour
- 6 cups milk
- Generous pinch of nutmeg
- 2 egg yolks, beaten
- ⅔ cups kefalograviera or Gruyere, grated
- Salt and pepper, to taste

INSTRUCTIONS

In a large pot, heat the olive oil over medium-high heat. Add the chopped onions and sauté, about 4-5 minutes. Add the garlic sauté for a minute. Add the beef, breaking it up with a wooden spoon. Cook until the mixture is almost dry. Add the grated tomato and sauté 2-3 minutes.

Add the tomato paste, sugar, cinnamon, allspice, and parsley. Add the stock or water and, season with salt and pepper. Bring to a boil. Cover and lower the heat to medium-low and simmer for 45-50 minutes, until it thickens and the juices evaporate.

Meanwhile, bring a large pot of salted water to a boil over high heat. Add the pasta and cook according to package directions. Drain pasta and set aside.

For the Béchamel Sauce:
Melt the butter in a deep saucepan over medium heat. Add the flour in stages, continuously whisking until the mixture is smooth. Whisk in the milk and continue whisking until thickened and creamy, about 12 to 15 minutes. Whisk in the nutmeg. Let the sauce cool for a minute or two, whisk in the lightly beaten egg yolks. Add the cheese and stir until incorporated. Season to taste. Preheat oven to 400°F.

Brush a 9x13 baking dish with olive oil. Place the noodles at the bottom of the dish. Add a ladle full of béchamel and half of the shredded cheese. Mix to combine. Add 2-3 tablespoons of béchamel sauce to the beef mixture and mix. Spread the beef mixture over the pasta. Pour the béchamel sauce over the beef, covering entire surface of dish. Sprinkle the rest of the cheese over the béchamel layer.

Place the dish in the oven and bake until golden on top and crisp around the edges, about 50-60 minutes. Remove it from the oven and let it rest for at least 30- 40 minutes before serving.

Lahanodolmades
Stuffed Cabbage

main plate

SERVES 4-6

INGREDIENTS

1 whole cabbage

½ lemon juice

STUFFING:

1 pound ground beef (or a mix of lamb and pork or beef and pork)

1 large onion, grated

½ bunch fresh dill, finely chopped

½ bunch fresh parsley, finely chopped

½ cup uncooked long grain rice

4 cups stock, plus more if needed

⅓ cup olive oil

Salt and freshly ground pepper, to taste

EGG LEMON SAUCE:

2 egg yolks

1 egg

Juice of 2 lemons

1 tablespoon cornstarch (optional)

INSTRUCTIONS

For the Cabbage:
Bring a large deep pot of water to a boil. Add the lemon juice. Meanwhile, discard the outer leaves of the cabbage. Tear the leaves off, one-by-one, taking care to keep each leaf intact. Wash each leaf thoroughly. Blanch the leaves several at a time for about 1 minute. The leaf should be soft. Take them out with a slotted spoon and place in a colander to drain. Repeat with the rest of the leaves and pour out the remaining water and set aside the pot. In a large bowl, combine the beef, onions, dill, parsley, rice, and mix until well combined. Set aside.

Separate the cabbage leaves 1-by-1 and remove any thick veins. On a flat surface lay the cabbage leaf vein side up with the stem end towards you. Place about 1-1 ½ tablespoons of the filling on the bottom center of the leaf. Do not overfill the rolls, as the rice will expand during cooking.

Fold the lower section of the leaf over the filling towards the center. Bring the two sides in towards the center then roll them up (not too tightly). If the cabbage leaf is too big, cut it in 2 or 3 smaller pieces. Continue with the remaining leaves and filling. Line the bottom of the pot with a few of the blanched cabbage leaves to prevent the cabbage rolls from burning. Place stuffed cabbage rolls, seam side down in the pan side by side in tight rows. Do not leave any gaps. When the first layer is complete, continue with a second and/or third layer. Try to fit as many in a single layer as possible. Pour enough stock to just cover the cabbage rolls. Season with salt and pepper and add the olive oil.

Place a heatproof plate over rolls with the back end of the plate facing you. This is done to keep the rolls in place while cooking and to prevent them from unwrapping. Cover and bring to a boil. Reduce the heat and simmer over a low heat until the rolls are nice and tender, approximately 1 hour. Turn off the heat, uncover the pot and remove the plate.

For the Egg and Lemon Sauce:
In a medium bowl, whisk egg yolks and egg until frothy. Whisk in the lemon juice, cornstarch, and set aside. Carefully take a few ladles of the cooking liquid from the pot and place it in a measuring cup with a spout.

Slowly drizzle the cooking liquid into the lemon/egg mixture while whisking constantly. Pour the lemon/egg mixture onto the cabbage rolls and swirl the pot to evenly distribute the sauce. Bring to a very gentle simmer over medium-low heat for just 1-2 minutes, making sure it does not come to a boil. Sauce will have slightly thickened. Remove from the heat. Taste and adjust the broth for seasoning.

Arrange the rolls onto individual plates, drizzle them with the sauce and garnish with lemon slices, fresh dill and some freshly ground pepper.

Youvetsi
Meat Stew with Orzo

main plate

SERVES 4-6

INGREDIENTS

½ cup olive oil, plus extra for sautéing

2 pounds lamb, beef, or meat of your choice, cut into small pieces

1 large onion, finely chopped

1 tablespoon tomato paste

¼ cup red wine

1 cinnamon stick

4-5 allspice berries or ¼ teaspoon ground allspice

Zest of half a lemon

3 fresh tomatoes, grated

½ teaspoon sugar

4 cups vegetable stock or water

1 pound orzo or hilopites (Greek square noodles)

Salt and pepper, to taste

Feta, for serving

INSTRUCTIONS

In a large dutch oven, heat the olive oil over medium-high heat. Season the beef with salt and pepper and brown half the meat for 4-5 minutes on all sides. Transfer the meat to a bowl and brown the second batch. Transfer the second batch to the bowl and set aside.

In the same pot, add the onion and sauté for 3-4 minutes. Add the tomato paste and let it cook for a minute. Pour in the wine, scraping up the brown bits stuck to the bottom of the pan. Add the cinnamon stick, allspice, lemon zest and let it sauté for 2 minutes.

Add the grated tomato, sugar, 2 cups of stock, season with salt and pepper and mix thoroughly. Return the meat back to the dutch oven and bring to a boil. Reduce heat to medium, cover, and allow the meat to simmer until nice and tender, about 45-50 minutes.

Remove the cinnamon stick and the allspice. Preheat the oven to 400°F.

Slowly pour the sauce and meat into a large roasting pan. Add the orzo and stir gently to distribute the ingredients evenly. Make sure that there is enough liquid for the orzo. If the orzo is not fully covered by the sauce, add as much as needed of the remaining stock to cover with an extra inch on top. Place in the oven and bake for 25 minutes. Let it rest for 10-15 minutes before serving.

Just before serving, taste and adjust seasonings to your liking. Serve warm with a sprinkle of feta cheese.

Notes: You can also replace the feta with a sprinkle of grated myzithra cheese. Do not over season, since myzithra cheese is very salty.

WorldwideGreeks.com **favorite**

Makaronia me Kima
Meat Sauce with Spaghetti

main plate

SERVES 4-6

INGREDIENTS

- **¼ cup olive oil**
- **1 large onion finely diced**
- **1 clove garlic minced**
- **2 pounds ground beef**
- **1 ½ tablespoons tomato paste**
- **½ cup red wine**
- **14 ounce can crushed tomato (or fresh grated)**
- **1 teaspoon sugar**
- **1 cinnamon stick**
- **3-4 allspice berries or ¼ teaspoon ground allspice**
- **⅓ bunch parsley, finely chopped**
- **⅔ cup veggie stock**
- **Salt and pepper, to taste**
- **1 pound spaghetti**
- **Myzithra or parmesan cheese, for serving**

INSTRUCTIONS

In a large pot, heat the olive oil over medium-high heat. Add the chopped onions and sauté, about 4-5 minutes or until translucent. Add the garlic sauté for a minute. Add the beef, breaking it up with a wooden spoon.

Cook until the mixture is almost dry. Add the tomato paste and sauté 1 minute. Pour in the wine, scraping up the brown bits stuck to the bottom of the pan. Add the tomato, sugar, cinnamon, allspice, parsley and season with salt and pepper.

Add the stock, season with salt and pepper. Bring to a boil. Cover and lower the heat to medium-low and simmer until it thickens and the juices evaporate, about 35-45 minutes. Taste and adjust seasonings to your liking. Remove cinnamon stick.

Meanwhile, bring a large pot of salted water to a boil over high heat. Add the pasta and cook according to package directions.

Drain pasta. Sprinkle in a good amount of myzithra (or parmesan) and toss to combine. Divide pasta among plates and spoon the Kima on the top. Sprinkle with remaining grated cheese.

Notes: Do not over season sauce, since the myzithra cheese is very salty.

WorldwideGreeks.com **favorite**

Gemista
Stuffed Vegetables

main plate

SERVES 4-6

INGREDIENTS

4 green bell peppers

8 medium-sized tomatoes

2 eggplants

5 potatoes

1 cup olive oil

2 medium onions, finely chopped

4 garlic cloves, minced

1 zucchini, grated

⅓ cup of mint, chopped

¼ cup parsley

2 tablespoons tomato paste

2 cups of rice

½ cup veggie stock

Salt and pepper, to taste

Feta cheese, for serving

INSTRUCTIONS

Wash the vegetables. Slice about ¼ inch off the top of the bell peppers. Save the tops for later. Remove any flesh or seeds. Set aside.

Slice about ¼ inch off the top of tomatoes. Save the tops for later. Carefully scoop out the pulp. Finely chop the pulp and set aside.

Cut a slice lengthwise off the eggplant and scoop out the inside flesh. Finely chop the flesh and set aside. Save the cut slices for later. Arrange all of the vegetables cut side up in a roasting pan. Wash and peel the potatoes. Slice the potatoes into 4 pieces each. Arrange nicely in the roasting pan in a single layer.

In a large sauté pan, heat ½ cup of oil over medium-high. Add the onions and sauté until translucent, about 5-6 minutes. Add the garlic and sauté for 1 minute. Add the eggplant flesh, zucchini, mint, parsley and tomato paste. Add the rice and sauté for 2-3 minutes. Add ¼ cup of stock, tomato pulp and any accumulated juices. Cook for 10 minutes.

Season with salt and pepper, stir thoroughly, and remove the pan from the heat. Preheat oven to 400°F.

Using a spoon, fill the tomatoes, eggplant and peppers ¾ of the way with the rice mixture. Cover each vegetable with its top. Add any of the leftover filling over the potatoes.

Add the remaining stock to the pan and drizzle with remaining olive oil. Add a little salt and pepper over the top of the vegetables. Cover with aluminium foil and place in the oven. Bake for about 1 hour and 15 minutes. Uncover halfway through cooking. Serve warm or straight out of the fridge with some briny feta cheese and lots of fresh bread.

Notes: Zucchini, when seasonally available, can also be a delicious addition to this dish. Simply cut, core and stuff.

Soutzoukakia Smyrneika
Meatballs in Tomato Sauce

main plate

SERVES 4-6

INGREDIENTS

MEATBALLS:

⅔ cup water

3 tablespoons vinegar

**6 slices white bread,
crust removed**

**2 pounds ground beef
(or a mix of half beef half pork)**

3 cloves garlic, minced

2 tablespoons olive oil

1 egg

2 ½ teaspoons cumin

Salt and pepper, to taste

**¼ cup olive oil plus extra
for frying**

Flour, for dredging

SAUCE:

1 onion grated

3 tablespoons olive oil

2 cups canned tomato puree

⅓ cup red wine

1 tablespoon cumin

Pinch cinnamon and sugar

Salt and pepper, to taste

INSTRUCTIONS

Pour the water and vinegar, in a medium bowl. Add the bread and soak for 2 minutes. Remove the bread from the soaking liquid and squeeze the bread as tightly as possible to remove as much liquid as you can.

In a large mixing bowl, combine beef, bread, garlic, oil, egg, cumin, season with salt, and pepper. Mix until combined.

Cover with plastic wrap and place in fridge for 20 minutes to rest.

Meanwhile, heat the olive oil in a large pot over medium heat. Add onion and sauté until translucent, about 5-7 minutes. Stir in the tomato puree, wine, cumin, cinnamon, sugar, season with salt and pepper and bring to a boil. Reduce heat to low and simmer for about 10 minutes.

Shape the meat mixture into 2 inch oblong shaped meatballs. Dredge in flour and set aside. Place a frying pan on medium heat. Add ½ inch of olive oil. When the oil shimmers add the meatball in a single layer and brown on all sides.

Place Soutzoukakia straight into the sauce and allow to simmer on low heat for an extra 15 minutes. Serve with white rice or Poure Patatas.

Notes: You can cook the meatballs directly in sauce and skip the frying steps for a lighter dish.

This dish can be made with pork or lamb and goes great with Lahanosalata.

WorldwideGreeks.com **favorite**

Kotopoulo Kokkinisto
Chicken Stew

main plate

SERVES 4-6

INGREDIENTS

4 tablespoons olive oil

1 chicken (about 3 pounds) chopped into small portions

Salt and freshly ground pepper, to taste

2 onions, finely chopped

1 garlic clove, minced

2 tablespoons tomato paste

¼ cup wine

2 ½ tablespoons red wine vinegar

3 fresh tomatoes, grated

1 tablespoon sugar

2 cinnamon sticks

4-5 whole cloves

2.5 cups veggie stock

8 ounces spaghetti or egg noodles

Myzithra or Parmesan cheese, for serving

INSTRUCTIONS

In a large dutch oven, add 4 tablespoons olive oil, and heat over medium-high heat. Season the chicken with salt and pepper and brown half the meat for 2-3 minutes on all sides. Transfer the meat to a bowl and brown the second batch. Transfer the second batch to the bowl and set aside. It's okay if it's not cooked through at this point.

In the same dutch oven, add the onions and sauté for 3-4 minutes. Add the garlic and sauté for a minute. Add the tomato paste and let it cook for a minute. Pour in the wine, scraping up the brown bits stuck to the bottom of the pan. Add the vinegar, tomatoes, sugar, cinnamon, cloves, stock and season with salt and pepper.

Return the chicken to the dutch oven and bring to a boil. Reduce heat to medium, cover, and allow the meat to simmer until nice and tender, about 45-50 minutes. Taste and adjust seasonings to your liking.

Meanwhile, bring a large pot of water to a boil. Season with a generous amount of salt. Cook the spaghetti until al dente according to the package directions. Drain thoroughly and set aside.

Serve the chicken over spaghetti or egg noodles. Spoon the tomato sauce on top and sprinkle with the grated cheese.

Notes: Do not over season the sauce, because the myzithra cheese is very salty.

Kotopoulo Lemonato Sto Fourno
Lemon Oregano Chicken

main plate

SERVES 4-6

INGREDIENTS

1 whole chicken, cut in pieces

6 large potatoes

2 tablespoons dried oregano

½ cup olive oil

Juice of 2 lemons

1 vegetable or chicken bouillon cube (or powder)

1 tablespoon mustard

2 cloves garlic, finely chopped

⅓ cup water

Salt and pepper, to taste

INSTRUCTIONS

Preheat the oven to 400°F.

Peel the potatoes, cut them into wedges and add them to a large roasting pan. In a medium bowl, whisk the oregano, olive oil, lemon juice, bouillion cube, mustard, garlic, season with salt, and pepper.

Pour half the marinade over the potatoes and mix until combined. Add the water into the pan. Set aside.

Place the chicken in a medium bowl. Pour the remaining marinade over the chicken stirring to coat. Place the chicken on top of the potatoes in the pan. Drizzle the remaining marinade over the chicken.

Cover the pan with aluminium foil and bake for 45 minutes. Uncover and bake for another 45 minutes, until nicely golden, and the potatoes are cooked through. Remove and serve immediately.

Biftekia me Patates
Beef Patties with Roasted Potatoes

main plate

MAKES 4-6

INGREDIENTS

POTATOES:

- 5-6 potatoes, peeled
- ⅓ cup olive oil
- Juice of 2 lemons
- 1 tablespoon mustard
- 2 cloves of garlic, finely chopped
- 2 tablespoons dried oregano
- 1 ½ vegetable bouillon cubes
- Salt and pepper, to taste
- ⅓ cup water

BURGERS:

- 5 slices bread, crust removed
- ½ cup milk
- 2 pounds ground beef
- 1 onion
- 1 clove of garlic
- ⅓ cup olive oil
- 1 ½ tablespoons oregano
- ¼ bunch parsley
- Salt & pepper

INSTRUCTIONS

Preheat the oven to 400°F.
Cut the potatoes into wedges and add them to a large roasting pan.
In a medium bowl, whisk the olive oil, lemon juice, mustard, garlic, oregano, bouillon cube, salt and pepper.

Pour half the marinade over the potatoes and mix until combined.
Set aside. Soak the bread in milk for five minutes.

Meanwhile, in a food processor, place the onion, garlic, olive oil, oregano, parsley, season with salt and pepper.

Squeeze the bread to remove most of the milk and then add it to the food processor. Process for about 1 minute. If it is too dry add 1 tablespoon of water a time. Transfer the mixture to a large bowl and add the beef.

Combine gently by hand until all the ingredients are completely combined. Cover the bowl with plastic wrap and refrigerate for half an hour.

Shape 10 burger patties and place them over the potatoes. Pour the remaining marinade over the patties. Add the water to the pan.

Cover the pan with aluminium foil and bake for 45 minutes. Uncover and bake for another 25-30 minutes, until nicely golden, and the potatoes are cooked through.

Notes: Serve with Greek Horiatiki salad and oregano.

WorldwideGreeks.com **favorite**

Giouvarlakia Avgolemono
Meatballs in Egg Lemon Sauce

main plate

SERVES 4-6

INGREDIENTS

MEATBALLS:

1 pound lean minced beef

⅓ cup long grain rice

½ cup finely chopped parsley

1 medium-sized onion, finely chopped

1 egg

3 tablespoons olive oil

3 tablespoons fresh dill, finely chopped

1 teaspoon salt

3 cups vegetable stock

Freshly ground pepper, to taste

EGG LEMON SAUCE:

2 eggs

Juice of 2 lemons

INSTRUCTIONS

In a large mixing bowl, stir together all the meatball ingredients. Place the mixture in the refrigerator to rest for 30 minutes. Shape about 18-20 meatballs and place them in large pot.

Add the stock and bring to a boil. The stock should be enough to cover the meatballs, add warm water if needed. Cover, and reduce heat to a gentle simmer. Simmer for about 30-35 minutes.

Beat the eggs in a bowl until frothy. Whisk in the lemon juice. In a slow steady stream, add 2-3 ladles of hot stock from the meatballs, whisking vigorously. Add 1 more ladle and whisk again until combined.

Tempering the egg will prevent it from separating and curdling when stirred into the sauce.

Stir the egg lemon sauce back into the pot with the meatballs. Simmer for about 2 minutes, until the sauce thickens. Serve with fresh bread and feta cheese.

seafood dishes

5.99
ΓΑΥΡΟΣ
ΕΛΛΗΝΙΚΟΣ
ΦΡΕΣΚΟΣ
1.99

The Spoils of the
Greek Seas

Seafood plays an important part in Greek cuisine. Thanks to the many islands and well-developed coastal areas, chefs and at-home cooks have access to the freshest seafood available all year round. For those living outside of Greece, seafood is often an afterthought when considering Greek cuisine. People enjoy the occasional Plaki, fried calamari or Kakavia but they don't rely on it as a mainstay in their diet. In Greece, seafood is a staple in a healthy Greek diet.

Seafood Variety

The most common types of seafood that you'll find in Greece are gavro (anchovies), marida (smelt), lavraki (sea bass), bakaliaro (cod) octopus, tsipoura (sea bream), shrimp, and squid. Because Greek cooking focuses on fresh ingredients, the type of fish that is listed in a recipe is a guideline rather than a requirement. Greek seafood recipes are versatile enough to allow for the 'catch of the day'. Most people learn how to prepare a few types of seafood dishes and use those to form the basis of their meals.

Popular Seafood dishes

Plaki is a popular style of baking fish with onions, lemons, tomatoes, capers and a variety of herbs. Typically, entire fish like cod is used, but any fish will do. Cooking the fish whole improves the flavor and keeps it moist. The meat found in the cheeks and tail are some of the most flavorful bites.

Kakavia, also referred to as fisherman's stew, is a common seafood dish. This delicacy is often times prepared as a meal on fishing boats using fresh catch. The stew is made by adding any seafood you have on hand to a pot with some broth or water, vegetables, tomatoes, and fresh herbs and letting it stew for a few hours. The result is a simple dish that is flavorful, hearty and perfect to serve with fresh bread for the broth.

Deep-fried seafood like squid and shrimp is also popular, as is pan-seared whole fish served with various vegetables and grilled or Marinated Octopus.

The Fishing Culture of Greece

Fishing is an essential part of the Greek economy, and a family tradition that ties the people of Greece to their heritage.

The abundance of sea surrounding Greece has made fish and seafood an important part of the Greek diet and economy. Ancient Greeks would set out on small wooden fishing boats called kaikia to fish for their families and trade. Greek people have held on to the ancient traditions of both boat making and fishing, passing on the knowledge and passion for the sea from generation to generation.

Lavraki Skaras
Grilled Branzino

seafood

SERVES 2-4

INGREDIENTS

2 whole bone-in branzino, cleaned

1 tablespoon olive oil

Salt and freshly ground black pepper

½ cup Ladolemono

1 tablespoon dried oregano, preferably Greek

LADOLEMONO

1 cup extra virgin olive oil

½ cup fresh squeeze lemon juice

1 tsp white pepper

1 tsp sea salt

INSTRUCTIONS

For the Branzino

Prepare a grill to medium-high heat. Brush fish with olive oil and season skin and cavity with salt and pepper. Place the fish in a fish grill basket. Grill fish, turning once, until the fish are white throughout, about 12 -15 minutes.

Transfer to a platter. Spoon Ladolemono on the grilled fish. Sprinkle some dried oregano as a garnish. Serve hot with Horta and a side of Patates Tiganites.

For the Ladolemono

Combine all the ingredients for the Ladolemono dressing into a jar. Close the lid tight and shake until emulsified. Adjust for seasoning.

COOKED
Eggplant in the oven
with feta cheese and
Chicken fillet with
in fresh tomato sauce
cooked in a clay
feta cheese, caper
rice with seafood
rice with meat
ILLED
tenderloin
steak
HOUS
Local white
White wine from
d wine from Crete
RITS
5, Whisky, Gin, Vodka 6 €
Liquer 100ml 5,5 €
9,5
9 €
9,5 €
8,5 €

Gavros Tiganitos
Fried Anchovies

seafood

SERVES 2-4

INGREDIENTS

1 pound fresh anchovies, washed

1 tablespoon salt

2 ½ cups all purpose flour

¾ cup cornstarch

½ cup olive oil for frying

1 lemon

INSTRUCTIONS

Place anchovies in a colander and strain for 10 minutes.

Meanwhile, in a large zip lock plastic bag, combine the salt, flour and cornstarch. Add the fish and coat well, being sure to shake off the excess.

In a medium sized skillet, heat the olive oil over medium-high heat. The oil should be approximately ½ inch deep. Once you see the oil shimmer add enough fish into the skillet side by side so that they are in one layer but not overcrowded.

Fry the fish until golden, turning once, about 3-5 minutes. Remove and place on paper towels to drain from excess oil.

Repeat with any remaining fish until they are all cooked. Serve the fried fish with lemon wedges and a side of Horta.

Htapodi Ksedato
Marinated Octopus

seafood

SERVES 4

INGREDIENTS

- **1 ½ pounds octopus, fresh or frozen and thawed**
- **1 cup white wine**
- **1 large bay leaf**
- **1 cup water**
- **3 tablespoons olive oil**
- **¼ cup vinegar**
- **¼ cup reserved cooking liquid**
- **Salt and pepper**
- **Dried oregano**

INSTRUCTIONS

Under cold, running water, remove and discard the head cavity, stomach, ink sac and eyes from the body of the octopus. Using a sharp knife remove the beak, at the bottom of the head where it joins the tentacles.

In a large pot, add the octopus, white wine, bay leaf and water. Bring to a boil over high heat. Reduce the heat to a simmer, cover, and cook until fork tender, about 50-60 minutes. When ready, reserve ¼ cup cooking liquid. Place the cooked octopus in a colander and set aside until cool enough to handle.

Cut the octopus into ½ inch-thick slices and place in a medium bowl. Add the vinegar, olive oil, reserved cooking liquid and toss to coat evenly. Cover and refrigerate for several hours or overnight.

When ready to serve, remove the octopus from the marinade. At this point it may have become slightly gel-like. Taste and adjust the seasoning, if necessary. Drizzle with more olive oil and sprinkle with oregano. Serve as a Mezze with Melitzanosalata and a perfectly cold ouzo.

Notes: Substitute a whole octopus for just tentacles.

Variation: Add cubed boiled potatoes

WorldwideGreeks.com **favorite**

Psari Plaki
Baked Fish

seafood

SERVES 3-4

INGREDIENTS

- 2 large tomatoes,
- 3 tablespoons olive oil
- 1 large onion, thinly sliced
- 2 cloves of garlic, thinly sliced
- ½ cup fresh parsley, finely chopped (more for garnish)
- 1 tablespoon capers, rinsed and drained
- ¼ teaspoon lemon zest
- Salt and Pepper
- 2 large potatoes, peeled and thinly sliced
- ⅓ cup olive oil
- 1 cup seafood stock
- 2 pounds cod (or other white fish like halibut or tilapia)
- 2 large tomatoes, sliced
- Salt and pepper to taste

INSTRUCTIONS

Preheat the oven to 375°F. Grease a 9x13 inch baking pan.
Place the tomatoes in a food processor fitted with a steel blade and pulse until nicely chopped.

In a large skillet, heat 3 tablespoons of olive oil over medium-high heat. Stir in the onions and sauté for 2 minutes. Add the garlic and sauté for 1 minute. Pour the tomatoes in the skillet and sauté for a minute. Add the stock, parsley, capers, lemon zest and season with salt and pepper. Simmer for 5 minutes.

Meanwhile, season the potatoes with salt and pepper. Lay the sliced potatoes in a single layer in the greased dish, slightly overlapping them if needed. Pour the sauce on top, drizzle with the remaining oil.

Cover the pan tightly with foil. Bake for 40-45 minutes. Remove the foil and place the fish on top of the potatoes. Layer the sliced tomatoes on top of the fish and season with salt and pepper.

Bake until fish becomes flaky, about 20 minutes. Garnish with parsley if desired.

Notes: Many Greek cooks substitute dill for the fresh parsley or combine the two. You can add bukovo or red pepper flakes, to make it more spicy.

Rizi me Calamari
Rice with Calamari

seafood

SERVES 4-6

INGREDIENTS

¼ cup olive oil

1 onion, finely diced

1 leek, sliced in rings

1 clove garlic, smashed

2 pounds calamari, chopped into round slices

Salt and freshly ground pepper

1 ½ cups dried arborio rice, rinsed

¼ cup Ouzo

½ cup rose wine

2 large tomatoes, grated

1 tablespoon tomato paste

½ tablespoon sugar

½ teaspoon bukovo or crushed red pepper, to taste

½ teaspoon salt

5 cups of seafood or vegetable stock

½ bunch parsley, finely chopped

INSTRUCTIONS

In a deep heavy-bottomed saucepan, heat the olive oil over medium-high heat. Add the onions and leeks and sauté, stirring occasionally, until softened, about 3-4 minutes.

Add the garlic and sauté for and additional minute.

Add the calamari, salt and freshly ground pepper and sauté, stirring, until it begins to curl, about 1-2 minutes.

Turn up the heat to medium-high and add the rice. Cook over moderately high heat, stirring vigorously with a wooden spoon. The rice will start to stick together, about 2-3 minutes.

Add the ouzo and wine and cook while stirring. When most of the alcohol has been fully absorbed, stir in the grated tomatoes, tomato paste, sugar, bukovo, salt and stock. Cover and reduce the heat to medium-low. Simmer for about 30 minutes.

Remove from heat and let it rest for about 5-10 minutes without uncovering it. Serve the rice hot, with freshly ground pepper and finely chopped parsley for garnish.

Astakomakaronada
Lobster Pasta

seafood

SERVES 4-6

INGREDIENTS

2 - 1 ¼ pound live lobsters or 1 pound claw, body, tail meat mixture

2 teaspoons olive oil

1 small onion

1 clove garlic

1 tablespoon tomato paste

¼ cup Metaxa 7 (Greek Cognac)

1 cup grated fresh tomato

1 ½ tablespoons butter

1 pound of spaghetti (Tagliatelle or Linguine)

Salt and black pepper to taste

1 tablespoon freshly parsley, chopped

INSTRUCTIONS

Bring a large pot of salted water to a boil. Place the lobster into the pot and wait for the water to return to a boil. Cook the lobster for about 8-9 minutes. Remove the lobsters from the pot and set aside to cool. Strain the cooking liquid and place the clear liquid back in the same large pot.

Over a large bowl (in order to catch any juices), remove the meat from the tails, claws, and knuckles. Chop the lobsters into small pieces and place in medium bowl. Strain the accumulated juices from the large bowl and set aside.

In a large pot or dutch oven, heat the olive oil over medium-low heat. Add the head and tail shells, stirring constantly. Add the onions and garlic and cook until they are translucent and garlic is softened but not brown, about 4 to 5 minutes. Mix the tomato paste into the pan and cook for a minute. Add the cognac and increase the heat to medium-high while continuing to stir.

Add the juices that you accumulated while cutting up the lobster and continue stirring to make a uniform sauce. Lower heat to a simmer and allow sauce to reduce by half, about 5 minutes.

Add the crushed tomato and let it cook over medium-low heat with the pan covered for 20 minutes (do not remove the shells or the roe, if any). At the end of cooking, add the butter and season with salt and pepper.

Meanwhile, boil the spaghetti in the pot with the reserved cooking liquid. Cook according to the package directions.

Lift the lid off of the sauce pot and remove the lobster shells. When the pasta has 2 minutes left to cook, add the lobster to the sauce and mix to combine. Taste and adjust the seasoning, if necessary. If the sauce is very thick, add a little water. Drain the pasta and add to the pot with the lobster sauce. Mix to combine and sprinkle with parsley.

WorldwideGreeks.com **favorite**

Aegean Kakavia
Aegean Fish stew

seafood

SERVES 4-6

INGREDIENTS

3 tablespoons olive oil

1 large onion, diced

1 clove garlic, minced

2 celery stalks, chopped

2 carrot stalks, sliced

2 large tomatoes, cored and chopped

½ pound potatoes, diced

1 bay leaf

4 cups organic seafood stock

1 cup clam juice

Salt and pepper, to taste

2 pounds fresh fish fillets, cleaned

1 lemon, juiced

½ bunch fresh, flat-leaf parsley, roughly chopped

Pinch of bukovo spice or ground red pepper flakes (optional)

1 loaf rustic bread, to serve

INSTRUCTIONS

In a large soup pot or dutch oven, heat the olive oil over medium-high heat. Stir in the onions, garlic, celery and carrots and cook for 5 minutes, Add the tomatoes, potatoes and bay leaf.

Stir in the stock, clam juice, salt and pepper. Bring it all to the boil, reduce to medium-low heat and simmer for 20 minutes. Taste and adjust the seasoning, if necessary.

Season fish pieces with salt and pepper, place them in the stew and simmer on low, covered, until fish is just cooked through, about 5-6 minutes. Stir in the lemon juice, parsley and bukovo (if desired). Check to make sure you have a good balance of acidity and seasoning.

Serve with chunks of rustic bread.

Notes: If possible, get fish from sustainable sources. Ask your fishmonger to clean the fish so that it is descaled and pin-boned.

vegetarian meals

Greek Olive Oil,
Liquid Gold

Olive oil is always present at the Greek table. Nearly every dish that Greek cooks prepare uses this highly prized oil. Greece is known as one of the largest producers of olive oil in the world, winning international awards year after year.

The Legend of the Olive Tree

According to legend, Athena, the Goddess of Wisdom, is responsible for giving Athens the olive tree as a gift. In the legend, Athena and Poseidon were in competition over who would have the new city-state named afterthem. Poseidon struck the ground with his staff and gave the Athenians the gift of flowing salt water. Athena struck the ground with her staff and it turned into an olive tree.

Since the olive tree provided wood, nourishment, and trade, Athena won the contest and became the patron goddess. The olive tree became a symbol of peace because of this victory and an important symbol of Greek culture and heritage.

Olive Oil in Greek Cuisine

Due to the abundance of olive oil in Greece, it is the main source of fat in the Greek diet. From sautéing, to baking, to dipping, this "liquid gold" is integrated in most dishes.

There is a style of Greek cuisine referred to as Ladera, which translates to 'in oil'. Ladera dishes are typically vegetarian meals of vegetables or beans baked in olive oil. Some traditional Ladera recipes include: Briam, Fasokalia, Gigantes and Aginares.
When using olive oil in Greek cuisine, it is important to make sure you use the right type of olive oil to maximize the flavor profile of your dish.
Extra virgin olive oil, which is easily distinguished by its green hue, should be used to enhance the flavor profile. It has a bold flavor that can give you a slight burning feeling in the back of your throat. Extra virgin olive oil is used in many dishes, dips, dressings and as a finishing oil.

Pure olive oil, or light olive oil, comes in shades of gold and is best used when frying or baking.

Medicinal Uses of Olive Oil

The Ancient Greeks explored the use of olive oil as medicine, and the tradition of it for healing is prevalent today in both the health and beauty industries. Olive oil is very high in antioxidants and has potent anti-inflammatory properties. It is used to prevent and treat many health issues such as digestive problems, high cholesterol and blood pressure, ear infection pain, arthritis, congestion and other respiratory complaints.

Briam
Roasted Vegetables

vegetarian

SERVES 4-6

INGREDIENTS

4 medium potatoes, sliced into ¼-inch rounds

1 pound eggplant, sliced into ¼-inch rounds

3 zucchinis, sliced into ¼-inch rounds

1 large onion, diced

2 medium ripe tomatoes, pureed

⅓ cup canned tomato puree

⅔ cup olive oil

4 cloves of garlic, finely chopped

⅓ cup chopped parsley

⅓ cup water

Salt and freshly ground pepper

INSTRUCTIONS

Preheat the oven to 400°F.

Place potatoes, eggplant, zucchini, and onion in a 9x13-inch baking dish, or preferably in a larger pan. Add the pureed tomatoes, tomato puree, olive oil, garlic, parsley, water, salt and freshly ground pepper. Toss together so that the vegetables are evenly coated.

Cover the pan with aluminium foil and bake for about 1 hour. Uncover the Briam, stir the vegetables and continue baking until the veggies are soft and charred and most of the liquid has evaporated, about 35-40 minutes.

Monitor the liquid levels and add a bit of water if veggies are not cooked through. Serve with briny feta cheese and lots of bread.

WorldwideGreeks.com **favorite**

Fasolakia Ladera
Braised Green Beans

vegetarian

SERVES 4-6

INGREDIENTS

⅓ cup olive oil

1 onion, finely chopped

1 clove garlic, finely chopped

1 ½ tablespoons tomato paste

1 ½ pounds green beans, washed & ends trimmed

3 potatoes, peeled and cut in large pieces

3 large ripe tomatoes, pureed

1 teaspoon sugar

Salt and pepper, to taste

Water or vegetable stock

½ bunch fresh parsley, minced

INSTRUCTIONS

In a large pot, heat the olive oil over medium-high heat. Add the onion and garlic, sauté for a minute. Add the tomato paste and sauté for a minute.

Add the green beans, potatoes and stir frequently to coat with tomato/oil, about 2-3 minutes. Add the pureed tomato and sugar. Season with salt and pepper. Add enough hot water so the beans and the potatoes are half covered.

Cover and lower the heat to medium and allow to simmer for 25 minutes.

Add the parsley and continue to cook for another 25 minutes or until beansare tender and water has reduced and thickened. Towards the last 10 minutes of cooking, shake the covered pot slightly to ensure even cooking and to make sure nothing sticks to the bottom of the pot.

Let it rest uncovered, for 10-15 minutes.

Just before serving, taste and adjust seasonings to your liking. Serve warm or at room temperature with feta cheese and fresh crispy bread.

Gigantes Plaki
Baked Giant Beans

vegetarian

SERVES 4-6

INGREDIENTS

1 pound dried gigantes or butter beans

⅓ cup extra virgin olive oil

1 onion, finely chopped

3 sprigs celery, finely chopped

2 garlic cloves, finely chopped

3 tablespoons tomato purée

4 large ripe tomatoes, grated (or 1- 14oz can crushed)

2 tablespoons chopped flat-leaf parsley

1 teaspoon sugar

1 tablespoon fresh lemon zest

Salt and Pepper, to taste

1 ½ cups reserved bean water

Crumbled feta cheese, for serving

INSTRUCTIONS

Soak the beans in a bowl full of salted water for 6-12 hours or overnight. Drain the water and add the beans to a pot. Add water and bring to a boil over medium high heat. Reduce heat to a simmer.

Simmer beans for an hour or until soft. When ready, drain beans reserving 1 ½ cup of water. Set aside.

Preheat oven to 350°F

In the same pot, heat the olive oil. Add onion, celery and sauté over medium heat for 5 minutes until translucent. Add garlic, and sauté for a minute.

Add the tomato purée and cook for 2 minutes. Add grated tomatoes, parsley, sugar, zest, salt and pepper and simmer for 3 minutes. Remove from heat. Add beans into the sauce. Gently stir to combine.

Transfer the bean mixture into a large ovenproof dish. Add the reserved water. Slowly stir with a wooden spoon.

Cover with aluminium foil. Bake for around 60-75 minutes, until the beans are softened.

Uncover and bake for an additional 15 minutes. At this point the beans should be tender, and the sauce will have thickened. Allow to slightly cool. Sprinkle with feta cheese just before serving.

Spanakorizo
Spinach Rice

vegetarian

SERVES 4-6

INGREDIENTS

- 1 pound fresh spinach
- ⅓ cup extra virgin olive oil
- 1 large onion, finely chopped
- 3 scallions, trimmed and sliced
- 1 leek, chopped
- 7 ounces fresh tomatoes, chopped
- 1 tablespoon tomato paste
- 3 cups vegetable stock
- ½ bunch fresh dill, snipped or chopped
- 1 cup medium grain rice
- Salt and pepper, to taste
- 1 or 2 fresh lemons, cut into wedges (for serving)

INSTRUCTIONS

Wash, rinse and drain the spinach thoroughly. Roughly chop.

In a large pot, heat ⅓ cup of olive oil over medium-high heat.
Add the onions, scallions, leek and sauté, stirring, for about 2 minutes.

Add the spinach in two batches stirring frequently, until wilted about 4-5 minutes. Stir in the tomatoes, tomato paste and stock. Add the dill, rice and bring to a boil. Cover and reduce heat on low.

Cook for 30-35 minutes until rice is tender and water is absorbed. Leave covered for 10 minutes. Season to taste. Sprinkle with feta and serve with lemon wedges and plenty of fresh bread.

WorldwideGreeks.com **favorite**

Papoutsakia Imam
Stuffed Eggplants

vegetarian

SERVES 4

INGREDIENTS

4 small eggplants

2 medium onions, sliced very thin

6 garlic cloves, finely chopped

1½ pounds tomatoes, peeled and grated

3 tablespoons canned tomato puree

¼ cup fresh parsley, finely chopped

Salt and pepper to taste

½ cup olive oil

¼ cup water

2½ teaspoons sugar

½ cup feta cheese, crumbled

INSTRUCTIONS

Preheat the oven to 450°F. Line a baking sheet with parchment paper and brush with olive oil. Arrange the rack in the middle of the oven.

Cut the eggplants in half lengthwise. Place on the baking sheet, skin side down, and bake for 20 minutes, until the outer skin begins to shrivel. Remove from the oven and transfer, cut side down, to a colander set in the sink. Allow to drain for 30 minutes.

Meanwhile, heat 3 tablespoons of olive oil in a large skillet over medium heat. Add the onions and sauté, stirring often, about 5-8 minutes.

Add the garlic, sauté for 30 seconds - 1 minute. Add the tomato puree and sauté for 30 seconds - 1 minute. Add the tomatoes, herbs, sugar and salt to taste. Cook for 5-6 minutes until juices have reduced. Remove from the heat and set aside.

Lower oven to 400°F. degrees.

Turn the eggplants over and place in a 9x13 pan, cut side up. Season with salt. Fill with the onion and tomato mixture, pressing down center with spoon to make room. Sprinkle with feta cheese.

In a small bowl, mix together the remaining olive oil, water and accumulated tomato juice from the skillet. Drizzle over and around the eggplants. Cover the pan with aluminium foil and bake for 25 minutes.

Uncover and bake for another 30-35 minutes, basting from time to time with the liquid in the pan. Add water to the pan if it becomes too dry.

The eggplants will turn out fairly flat and the liquid in the pan slightly caramelized. Remove from the oven and allow to cool in the pan at least 40-45 minutes before serving. Serve with extra feta cheese and lots of fresh bread.

STAUB
STAUB

Aginares a la Polita
City-Style Artichokes

vegetarian

SERVES 4-6

INGREDIENTS

⅓ cup olive oil

1 onion, thinly sliced

5 green onions chopped, green part included

1 clove of garlic minced

3 medium carrots, sliced into thin rounds

6 small potatoes, peeled and cut in half

10 frozen or fresh artichoke hearts, cut in half

1 tablespoon flour

2-3 tablespoons fresh lemon juice

⅓ bunch dill, chopped

Vegetable broth or water

Salt and pepper, to taste

INSTRUCTIONS

In a large pot, heat the olive oil over medium-high heat. Add the onion, green onion and sauté for 2-3 minutes.

Add the garlic and sauté for a minute. Add carrots, potatoes and continue to sauté the vegetables another 5 minutes. Add the artichokes and sauté for 4-5 minutes, until light golden.

Add the flour, the lemon juice, dill, and enough broth, to come halfway up the sides of the artichokes.

Stir and reduce to medium-low heat. Cover and simmer for about 25-30 minutes or until the carrots and potatoes are fork tender.

Monitor the liquid levels and add a bit of water if needed.

Season with salt and freshly ground black pepper to taste. Cover and simmer an additional 10 minutes or until the artichokes are tender.

Serve with lemon wedges and a drizzle olive oil, accompanied with lots of fresh bread.

sides

από το
ΜΠΑΧΑΡΙΚΑ
Χαλβάς Ξάνθης
1.90

The Grains of Greek Cuisine

When most of us think about the grains that are used in Greek cooking, we mostly think of the rice dishes, breads, and forms of pasta that are typically used today. However, the traditional Greek diet has grains that many of us don't use anymore – but they are still an integral part of the cuisine in Greece, especially in some of the more remote areas. Some of the grains that are part of the traditional Greek diet include the following:

BARLEY
The use of barley goes back to the ancient times during the Hippocrates and Homer era. In ancient times, barley was valuable and was used by Hippocrates to treat sick people. Barley still finds its way into the Greek kitchen when making Cretan rusks, barley Greek salad, and Greek country bread. The country bread is delicious with Extra Virgin olive oil, Cretan cheese, and fresh tomatoes.

CORN
Corn was not eaten in ancient Greece, but rather came from the Americas in modern times. It has become a conventional dish in Greece and is now a part of the traditional diet. In some parts of Greece, a dried and coarsely ground corn meal, similar to polenta, is eaten. The resulting dish, called katsimaki, is a comforting, wholesome food that is served warm and often topped with feta cheese. Corn meal is also used to create savory pies called bobota that are rich with cheese, greens, and other ingredients.

RICE
Rice is commonly used in Greek dishes such as Dolmades, Rizogolo, Spanakorizo, and Pilafi. However, like corn, rice wasn't present in the Greek diet in Ancient times – it is a relatively modern addition.

SEMOLINA
Semolina is commonly used in making pasta and various bread types. Semolina originates from durum wheat and is common in the Mediterranean. The grain is used in dishes like Greek halva which is popular in Greece. It is also used in making Galaktoboureko.

WHOLE WHEAT BERRIES
Whole wheat berries are used to make koliva in the Greek Orthodox Church. Koliva is a mixture of wheat berries and other ingredients such as raisins, almonds, walnuts and currants. The mixture is molded, covered with confectioners' sugar and presented on a silver tray. The koliva are brought to church for memorial services where it is used to symbolize rebirth and death. The use of wheat berries in koliva symbolizes everlasting life.

Grains play a vital role in Greek cuisine, and there are a variety to choose from in your experimentation with Greek cooking.

Patates Lemonates
Lemon Potatoes

sides

SERVES 6-8

INGREDIENTS

4 large potatoes, peeled and cut into ¼- ½-inch-thick wedges

½ cup olive oil

4 garlic cloves, minced

2 teaspoons chopped fresh oregano leaves, or 1 teaspoon dried

¼ cup fresh lemon juice

1 teaspoon salt

½ teaspoon freshly ground black pepper

½ cup chicken stock

INSTRUCTIONS

Preheat the oven to 400°F.

Place the potatoes in a single layer in a 13-x-9-inch baking pan (or larger) and pour the olive oil over them. Add the garlic, dried oregano, lemon juice, salt and pepper and toss well to coat with the oil. Add the stock in between the gaps created by the potatoes.

Cover with aluminium foil and place in the oven. Bake, for 30 minutes.

Uncover and turn the potatoes twice. Continue baking until they are fork tender, lightly golden, and have begun to crisp, about 30 minutes.

WorldwideGreeks.com **favorite**

Patates Tiganites
Fried Potatoes

sides

SERVES 6

INGREDIENTS

4 medium potatoes, peeled and cut lengthwise into ¼-inch-thick sticks

Olive oil, for frying

Sea salt, to taste

INSTRUCTIONS

Place the potatoes in a large bowl of water and, using your hands, stir them for a minute. Drain and repeat the process 2 more times. On the last time do not drain and let them soak for 40 minutes.

Transfer the potatoes to a colander and shake off the excess water. Blot with paper towels to dry them.

In a deep frying pan, heat 1 to 1 ½ inches of oil over medium-high heat. Place as many potatoes as will fit in 1 layer in the skillet. Fry over high heat for 2 minutes. Stir and turn the potatoes over, and cook until golden and crisp, another 3 to 4 minutes. Remove the potatoes from the oil and drain on paper towels.

Repeat, allowing the oil to reheat between batches, until all the potatoes are fried. Sprinkle with sea salt over the potatoes and toss to coat. Serve right away.

WorldwideGreeks.com **favorite**

Poure Patatas
Mashed Potatoes

sides

SERVES 4-6

INGREDIENTS

2 pounds Yukon Gold potatoes, peeled and cut into 2-inch cubes

2 bouillon cubes

½ cup cooking liquid (or milk), plus more as needed

½ cup extra virgin olive oil

1 garlic clove, smashed

Salt and pepper, to taste

¼ cup fresh flat-leaf parsley, chopped

INSTRUCTIONS

Fill a large pot with cold water. Add the potatoes, bouillon cubes and bring to a boil over high heat. Cook potatoes until very soft and tender. You will know they are tender when a skewer or knife can easily penetrate the center of the potatoes, about 20 to 22 minutes.

When ready, drain potatoes, reserving 1 cup of water as cooking liquid. Set aside.

Meanwhile, in a small pot, heat the olive oil and garlic over low heat for 4-5 min, and set aside.

Return potatoes to the pot and mash them with a potato masher. With a wooden spoon, stir in the warm olive oil. Add enough cooking liquid to make the potatoes creamy. Season generously with salt and several grinds of black pepper.

Just before serving, check the consistency of the potatoes. If too thick, add enough cooking liquid to make the potatoes creamy. Mix in the parsley. Taste and adjust seasonings.

To keep the potatoes warm, place the bowl over simmering water for up to 30 minutes.

Pilafi
Rice Pilaf

sides

SERVES 4-6

INGREDIENTS

1 cup long-grain white rice

1 tablespoon olive oil (or butter)

½ yellow onion, diced

1 garlic clove, smashed

1¾ cups water

1 vegetable bouillon cube

Salt and pepper, to taste

INSTRUCTIONS

Place the rice in a strainer and rinse it thoroughly under cool running water. The water running through the rice will look milky, but slowly it will become clear. Set aside.

In a large sauté pan, heat the olive oil over medium-high heat. Add the onion, garlic and cook until the onion is translucent and soft.

Add the rice to the pan and stir thoroughly until the grains are coated with the oil. Continue to cook, until the tips of the rice turn translucent and the rice smells fragrant and toasted, stirring often.

Stir in the water and vegetable bouillon cube, bring to a boil over high heat, cover, reduce the heat to medium-low and simmer until tender for 18 minutes. Let the rice rest off the heat for 5-6 minutes. Do not lift the lid or the rice will not cook evenly.

Open the lid and gently stir the rice to loosen the bottom and separate the grains.

Season with salt and pepper if needed. Transfer to a serving bowl and serve.

Notes: You can substitute the water and veggie cube with 1¾ cups chicken broth, vegetable broth, water, or a mix of water and broth.

Variation: Mushroom Oregano Rice Pilaf: Slice 8 ounces of button mushrooms or white mushrooms and a few sprigs of fresh oregano and cook them along with the diced onion until golden.

Horta
Wild Greens

sides

SERVES 4

INGREDIENTS

1 large bunch wild greens, dandelion, wild spinach, beetroot leaves, or amaranth (vleeta)

⅓ cup extra virgin olive oil

1-2 lemons

2 teaspoons salt

INSTRUCTIONS

Bring a large pot of water to a boil.

In the meantime, cut off and discard any bruised leaves or stems from the greens. Wash your greens thoroughly in the sink a few times over, to rinse away any soil.

Carefully submerge the greens into the boiling water and cover until it starts to boil again. Uncover your pot, and reduce your heat to medium. Stir the Horta a few times.

Boil for about 10-15 mins or until the thickest parts of the stems are tender. Be careful not to over boil.

Strain and place in serving dish. Drizzle the greens with the extra virgin olive oil and lemon juice. Season with salt. Serve as a side or an appetizer with plenty of fresh bread.

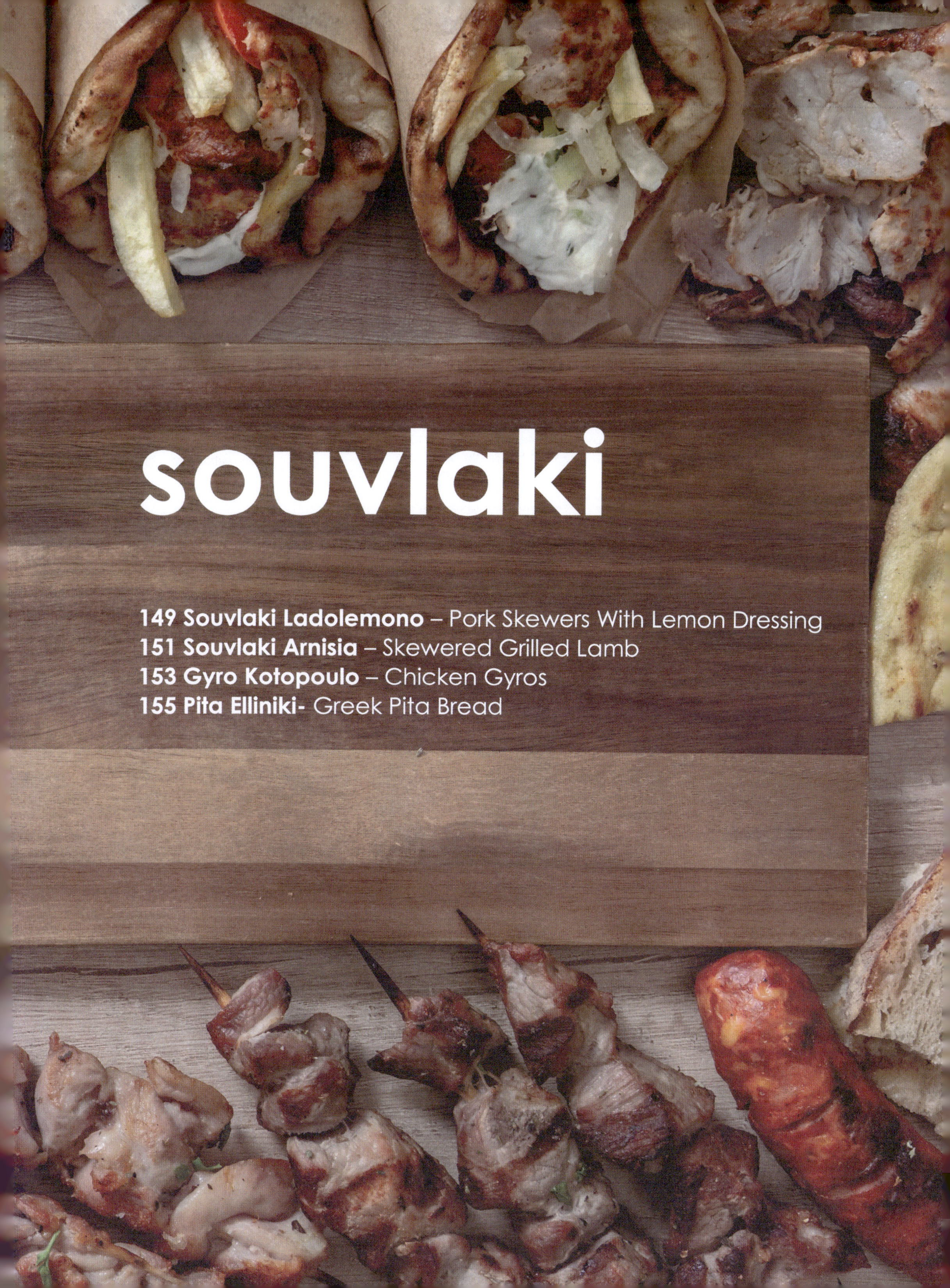

souvlaki

149 Souvlaki Ladolemono – Pork Skewers With Lemon Dressing
151 Souvlaki Arnisia – Skewered Grilled Lamb
153 Gyro Kotopoulo – Chicken Gyros
155 Pita Elliniki- Greek Pita Bread

KOSMIKON
GYROS
KEBAB
SOUVLAKI
MOUSAKA
MIXED GRILLED
MIXED SEAFOOD
KOSMIKON
GYROS
SOUVLAKI
KEBAB
MOUSAKA
SPAGHETTI
SEAFOOD
FRESH FISH

Souvlaki, The World-Famous
Street Food

Souvlaki, which translates to "little skewer", is a well-known and tasty Greek dish. The name originates from the Greek word souvla, which means "skewer". Whether eaten as a street food wrapped in a pita, or plated with potatoes and other vegetables, Souvlaki is a popular choice amongst locals and tourists.

A common street food, souvlaki is a skewer of meat that can be enjoyed in various ways including:

KALAMAKI - When ordering a kalamaki, you will be served a skewer of meat in a small bag with a slice of lemon and piece of fresh bread.

TYLIKTO - If you ask for your Souvlaki tylikto, you will receive a handheld wrap. A warm Greek pita is smothered with Tzatziki and filled with skewer meat. Toppings can include tomato, onions and fried potatoes. Some regions swap out the tzatziki and onions with a yellow mustard sauce and lettuce. Ktipiti, Russian salad, and Melitzanosalata are other options used.

MERIDA - Translated, merida means "portion". A merida of souvlaki is often ordered when sitting to enjoy a meal. A skewer (or 2) of meat is served on a plate accompanied by pita bread, potatoes and other vegetables.

Pork is the most common meat used in Greek Souvlaki, but other options such as chicken, beef and lamb are always available.

History of Greek Souvlaki

Historically, the use of spits and skewers for cooking in Greece stretches back to the Bronze Age. Excavations on the island of Santorini uncovered stone cooking supports used to prepare souvlaki before the Thera volcanic eruption in the 17th century BC. Archaeologists also uncovered "souvlaki trays," and spit supports at various sites in Mycenae.

Several authors in Greek literature also refer to meat being roasted on spits, including Aristotle and Homer in the Iliad.

Modern souvlaki didn't become common in Greece until after World War II. In the 1960s, sellers brought Souvlaki skewers to the general public as a quick meal option. The term "souvlaki" first appeared in print in 1942.

Souvlaki Ladolemono
Pork Skewers With Lemon Dressing

souvlaki

MAKES 8 SKEWERS

INGREDIENTS

SKEWERS:

¾ cup olive oil

2 tablespoons dried oregano plus some extra for garnish

1 lemon zested and juiced

2 garlic cloves, crushed

1 ½ teaspoon paprika

Salt and pepper

1 ½ pounds pork shoulder, or boneless skinless chicken breast, cut into bite size chunks

8 wooden skewers soaked in water

LADOLEMONO:

1 lemon juiced

1 tablespoon dried oregano

⅓ cup Extra virgin olive oil

ASSEMBLY:

Pita bread, or other flatbreads, warmed on the grill

1 red onion, sliced

Lettuce, shredded

2 tomatoes, sliced

INSTRUCTIONS

If using wooden skewers, soak them in a tray of water to stop them from burning. In a mixing bowl, whisk together the olive oil, oregano, lemon zest, lemon juice, garlic and paprika. Season with salt and pepper. Place the pork into the bowl and toss to coat. Marinate and refrigerated, at least 1 hour or overnight.

Prepare a grill for direct grilling over medium-high heat (about 400°F). Remove the pork from the marinade. Allow the excess marinade to drain off. Thread the meat onto the skewers (about 4 to 5 pieces per skewer). Season the pork with salt and freshly ground black pepper.

Grill, turning the skewers occasionally, until the pork is well marked and cooked through, 7 to 8 minutes total. The internal temperature of the pork should reaches 145°F. Drizzle the ladolemono over the meat before serving. Sprinkle with oregano. Serve with onion, lettuce, tomato, pita and tzatziki.

For The Ladolemono Dressing:
In a dressing container or jar add the lemon juice, oregano and olive oil. Shake the container until a creamy dressing forms and pour over the souvlakia, right as they come out of the grill.

Notes: Ladolemono can be made in advanced and kept in the refrigerator. This marinade is simple, it's got good taste and you can certainly apply it to chicken or lamb souvlaki.

Make this recipe into a souvlaki plate by adding Patates Tiganites.

If you don't have a grill, do not thread the meat onto skewers. Simply cook the meat in a dry cast-iron skillet over high heat for 3 minutes, until it is nicely charred and crispy around the edges.

WorldwideGreeks.com **favorite**

Souvlaki Arnisia
Skewered Grilled Lamb

souvlaki

MAKES 12 SKEWERS

INGREDIENTS

⅓ cup olive oil; more for drizzling

1 cup red wine

1 large red onion, grated

2 garlic cloves, finely minced

3 teaspoon dried oregano or 3 tablespoons fresh oregano chopped

1 tablespoon rosemary, chopped

Salt and freshly ground black pepper

2-½ pounds boneless leg of lamb, trimmed and cut into 1-½-inch cubes

2 large green bell peppers, cut into 1-½-inch pieces

2 tomatoes cut into 1-½-inch cubes

2 onions cut into 1-½-inch pieces, layers separated

Tzatziki, for serving

Lemon wedges, for serving

Pita breads (optional)

Fresh oregano, for serving (optional)

INSTRUCTIONS

In a medium bowl, whisk the olive oil, red wine, grated onion, garlic, oregano, rosemary, 2 teaspoon salt, and ¾ teaspoon pepper. Put the lamb and vegetables in two separate large zip lock plastic bags. Divide the marinade between the bags, squeeze the air out and close tightly. Refrigerate for at least 6 hours or overnight.

If using wooden skewers, soak them in a tray of water to stop them from burning.

Prepare a grill for direct grilling over medium-high heat (about 400°F -450°F). Remove the lamb and vegetables. Allow the excess marinade to drain off. Loosely thread the lamb onto skewers, alternating with pieces of green pepper, onion and tomato.

If there are leftover vegetables, thread them onto a separate skewer. Generously season the skewers with salt and pepper.

Grill, turning the skewers occasionally, until the lamb is well marked and cooked through, 6 minutes for medium-rare lamb or to your desired doneness. Let the souvlaki rest for a 5-6 minutes before serving.

Transfer the skewers to a large serving platter. Sprinkle with fresh oregano. Serve with the tzatziki, onion tomatoes and lemon wedges. If serving with pitas, grill the pitas lightly or warm them on the grill for 2 to 3 minutes.

Gyro Kotopoulo
Chicken Gyros

souvlaki

SERVES 4-6

INGREDIENTS

2 pounds chicken thigh fillets

¼ cup wine

¼ cup olive oil

2 garlic cloves, minced

Juice of a lemon

2 teaspoons dried oregano

1 ½ teaspoon sweet paprika

1 teaspoon salt

1 teaspoon pepper

GYRO:

2 sliced tomatoes

5 onions, sliced into half moons

Salt and pepper

SERVE:

Tzatziki

4 to 6 pita breads

6 square pieces of Parchment baking paper or tin foil to wrap around the Gyro.

INSTRUCTIONS

In a large mixing bowl, add the chicken, wine, ½ the olive oil, garlic, lemon, oregano, sweet paprika salt and pepper and mix well to combine. Cover and refrigerate for at least 30 minutes or up to 3 hours.

In a large skillet, heat the remaining olive oil over a medium heat. Remove the chicken from the marinade discarding the marinade. Place the chicken in the pan in batches and cook for 4-5 minutes on each side. Chicken should be cooked through and golden brown. Cooking time will depend on the size of each piece. Remove the chicken from the pan and place on a plate.

Build the gyros:
Warm pita bread. Slice the chicken into thin strips. Take a piece of pita bread and place on parchment baking paper or foil. Place heaping tablespoon(or more) of tzatziki, then the chicken and last the veggies. Wrap the pita with the parchment paper, twisting the bottom to ensure it is closed. Enjoy!

Notes: Another option is to grill the chicken instead of pan frying. You can also skewer pork, lamb or chicken souvlaki and grill as well.

WorldwideGreeks.com **favorite**

Pita Elliniki
Greek Pita Bread

souvlaki

MAKES 8-10 PITA

INGREDIENTS

1 cup lukewarm water

½ cup lukewarm milk

1½ teaspoon active dry yeast

1 ½ teaspoon sugar

3 tablespoons olive oil

1 teaspoon sea salt

3 ¾ cup all-purpose flour

Flour for rolling

INSTRUCTIONS

In the bowl of a stand mixer fitted with a dough hook attachment, add the water, yeast, and the sugar. Mix on low speed until combined. Allow the yeast to bloom, about 5-7 minutes.

Meanwhile, in a separate bowl, combine the flour and the salt. Set aside. Pour milk and 2 tablespoons olive oil in the yeast mixture. Mix on medium speed until blended. Add flour and mix on low speed until a dough mass forms, about 2-3 minutes. Scrape the sides and bottom of the bowl and continue mixing for 2 minutes. Cover the bowl with damp towel allow it rise in a warm spot for about 30 minutes or doubled in size.

Portion and shape the dough into eight even pieces and place on a lightly oiled baking tray. Set aside.

Place one ball of dough on a lightly floured surface and roll each ball into an 8 inch round. It should be about ¼ inch thick. Allow to rest for 10 minutes before baking.

Using a large fork pierce the dough all over, making sure you do not pierce right through.

Line a large plate with a clean cotton kitchen towel.

Spray a seasoned cast-iron skillet with remaining oil and heat over medium-high heat until hot. Cook the pita on the pan for 1-2 minute. Pita will start to puff up
and get a nice golden color. Flip and cook the other side.

Place the pita bread on the plate and cover tightly with aluminium foil. This will ensure that the pita will stay moist, fresh and malleable.

Repeat with remaining dough balls. Serve warm or allow to cool underneath the aluminium foil.

Notes: If the dough resists the stretching, let it relax for a few minutes and then try rolling it again.

Store the pita bread in a sealed plastic bag for 3-4 days. You can also store some cooked pita bread in the freezer for later use.

dessert

The Natural Sweetness of Greek Honey

Honey has been used as a sweetener since Ancient Greece. Greek honey has been harvested for hundreds of years due to its sweet flavor and medicinal, nutrient-rich characteristics, indicating that humans have long enjoyed a sweet treat. Although Greek honey has only become popular abroad in recent years, it has a long history of being regarded as the finest in the world. This is because of its nutritious value and clean, sweet taste.

Honey from Greece comes from beekeepers all around the country who follow age-old methods. The information is passed down from parent to child and has become an integral component of the cuisine and culture. Like the flowers they pollinate, honeybees do well in Greece's temperate environment.

Popular types of Greek honey include the following:

THYME
Bees that are fed thyme, make less honey overall. This is why thyme honey is rare and so highly regarded in Greece. The honey has a light color and a strong herbal aroma. Thyme honey is good for coughs and sore throats due to its anti-inflammatory and anti-bacterial properties.

PINE
Pine honey accounts for roughly 65 percent of Greece's total honey production. Its mahogany hue belies the abundance of potassium, phosphorus, iron, magnesium, and sodium that make up its mineral components. Compared to other Greek honey, this honey contains the highest concentration of antioxidants.

BLOSSOM
Blossom honey is sweeter and more subtle than typical honey because it's made from orange blossoms and wildflowers. The faint orange and floral scent makes this the most popular type of honey for Greek desserts.

HEATHER
Heather honey is produced in early fall, when temperatures are still mild enough for heather to bloom. The consistency is spreadable and thick despite its dark, crimson color and practically solid state. Heather honey is high in antioxidants and antibacterial effects.

CHESTNUT
Chestnut honey is one of the rarest in Greece. This is a unique type of honey with a pleasant and faint bitterness. It is high in iron and is said to increase blood circulation and help in lowering of cholesterol.

Genuine Greek honey is an essential ingredient when preparing Greek dishes. After all, using local honey offers your meals a unique flavor that cannot be replicated with honey from another country. You should also pick Greek honey that blends well with the food.

Baklava
Phyllo Walnut Pastry

dessert

**MAKES 12 LARGE
OR 24 SMALL PIECES**

INGREDIENTS

FILLING:

7 ounces walnuts

3 tablespoons sugar

¼ teaspoon salt

1 ½ tablespoons cinnamon

¼ teaspoon ground cloves

¼ cup plain breadcrumbs

1 pound melted unsalted butter

1 pound phyllo dough sheets (9"x13") brought to room temperature

****Purchase phyllo sheets in smaller size (9"x13"). If only larger box such as 14"x18" available, cut sheets in half and use all of them.**

SYRUP:

3 cups sugar

1 ¾ cups water

3 tablespoons honey

1 cinnamon stick

3 whole cloves

1 lemon, cut in half

INSTRUCTIONS

For the filling:
In a food processor, combine the walnuts, sugar, salt, cinnamon, clove, breadcrumbs and process. The mixture will look like wet sand and small pebbles. Transfer the mixture to a medium bowl and set aside.

For the Assembly:
On a clean work surface, gently unroll the phyllo and trim the sheets into rectangles sized a little less than 9x13 inches. It should fit nicely into the baking dish. Cover the phyllo with plastic wrap and a kitchen towel to prevent it from drying out.

Brush the bottom of a 9x13 baking dish/pan with melted butter. Add the phyllo, 1 sheet at a time, drizzling with 2 to 3 teaspoons of the butter after every sheet. When you get to the 3rd sheet, sprinkle a little less than a handful of the filling, spreading it as evenly as possible. Add another sheet of phyllo and repeat the same process of layering the phyllo, butter and filling until the filling is used.

Finish the layering as you started with 3 more layers of phyllo, buttering after every one. Do not butter the top layer. Place the baklava in the freezer for 15 minutes in order for the butter to harden.

Preheat the oven to 325°F.

Cut the baklava in 12 squares, cutting all the way through the layers. Next, cut each square diagonally into two triangles(optional). If any butter remains, spoon it into the cut lines. Bake the baklava for 90 minutes. The top should be golden brown, and you should hear it bubbling. Meanwhile, 10 minutes before the baklava is done, start making the syrup.

For the syrup:
In a small saucepan, combine the sugar, water, honey, cinnamon stick. Half squeeze the lemon, and place the lemon into the water as well. Bring to a boil over medium heat. Immediately, reduce the temperature to low heat, and simmer, uncovered, for 5 minutes. Take the baklava out of the oven. Using a ladle, drizzle a ladleful of the hot syrup all over the hot balava. Allow the baklava to cool completely before serving, (at least 3 hours or overnight).

WorldwideGreeks.com **favorite**

Galaktoboureko
Custard and Phyllo Pastry

dessert

MAKES 12 LARGE OR 24 SMALL PIECES

INGREDIENTS

PASTRY:

1 package phyllo

1 cup melted unsalted butter

FILLING:

5 cups milk

1 cup sugar, divided

2 teaspoons vanilla

4 eggs plus 2 yolks

¾ cup fine semolina

5 tablespoons butter

SYRUP:

3 cups of sugar

1 ¾ cup of water

¼ cup honey

¼ cup cognac

1 lemon peel

Juice of half a lemon

1 cinnamon stick

INSTRUCTIONS

For the syrup:
In a small saucepan bring the sugar, water, honey, cognac, cinnamon stick, lemon peel and lemon juice to a boil, stirring until the sugar is dissolved. Boil without stirring for 10 minutes, then remove from the heat. Set aside.

For the filling:
Pour milk and half the sugar into a medium sauce pan and bring to just below boiling point. Remove from heat. In a large bowl, lightly whisk eggs, egg yolks and remaining sugar together. Stir in semolina.
In a small steady stream pour in about half of the of hot milk, whisking constantly. Add remaining milk to the bowl whisking constantly.

Return the milk/egg mixture back into pot and simmer over a low heat, while constantly whisking, for about 10 minutes. The mixture will be smooth and thick. Remove from heat, add vanilla and butter and whisk until well combined. Place a piece of saran wrap on top of the custard filling and set aside.

Preheat the oven to 375°F. Brush a 9x13 ovenproof dish or baking pan with melted butter.

Unroll the phyllo sheets and lay them flat. Working quickly, place 1 phyllo dough off center in the pan and let the edges hang over the sides. Brush the top sheet with butter taking care not to brush over the hanging sides. Place another phyllo on the other side, letting the edges hang over the sides. Brush the top sheet with butter taking care not to brush over the hanging sides. Continue on with this process until you have used half of the phyllo sheets.

Pour custard into the pan, smooth out evenly and fold the overhanging phyllo over the filling. Continue to layer remaining phyllo sheets over the custard mixture. Trim the overhang and with the pastry brush push the edges into the sides so they disappear. Score 12 even pieces. Be careful not to cut all the way through. Brush the top with any remaining butter and sprinkle with a little water.

Bake for 45-60 minutes until the top is golden and crisp.Remove from the oven and spoon the cold syrup over the hot pie. Allow pastry to cool and absorb the syrup, and serve warm or at room temperature.

WorldwideGreeks.com **favorite**

Pasta Flora
Apricot Jam Tart

dessert

MAKES 8 PIECES

INGREDIENTS

1 cup plus 2 tablespoons unsalted butter

1 cup powdered sugar

1 teaspoon salt

1 egg

4 cups flour

1 teaspoon baking powder

1 teaspoon vanilla

½ shot of cognac

1½ jars apricot jam

INSTRUCTIONS

In a stand mixer fitted with a paddle attachment, mix together the butter, sugar and salt until light and fluffy. Start off at a slow speed and gradually increase speed.

Add the egg and continue beating until completely combined. Decrease to slow speed and add baking powder, vanilla, and cognac. Gradually add the flour 1 cup at a time, until no longer sticky.

Place the dough out onto a clean work surface and gather it together into a tight ball. Knead by hand for 1-2 minutes. Make a ball out of dough, wrap the dough tightly in plastic wrap and press it down to make a disk about 1 inch thick. Refrigerate for at least 1 hour before using.

Place ¾ of the dough in between two sheets of parchment paper. Roll it out with a rolling pin, until it is slightly larger than the size of a tart pan.

Remove the top sheet of parchment paper and invert the dough onto the 10-11 inch round tart pan. Press the dough into the tart pan evenly. Trim the edges all around, and set them aside. Spread the jam evenly (or as much jam as you prefer) over the dough.

Take the remaining ¼ of the dough and dough scrapes, and form long strips placing them in a latticework pattern on top of the jam.

Preheated the oven to 350°F.

Beat the egg with a tablespoon of water in a small bowl, and brush it over the dough.

Bake on the middle oven rack for about 25 minutes or until golden brown.

WorldwideGreeks.com favorite

Koulourakia
Greek Butter Cookies

dessert

MAKES 40 COOKIES

INGREDIENTS

4 ounces unsalted butter

1 ounce margarine

¾ cup granulated sugar

2 eggs

3 tablespoons milk

½ tablespoon bakers' ammonia (or baking powder)

2 tablespoons orange juice

¼ teaspoon of baking soda

Zest from ¼ of an orange

1 pinch salt

½ tablespoon vanilla

1 pound all-purpose flour, sifted

INSTRUCTIONS

Position a rack in the center of the oven and preheat to 375°F. Line two baking sheets with parchment paper.

In a stand mixer fitted with paddle attachment (or a large bowl with a handheld electric mixer), beat the butter, margarine and sugar at low speed, for 10-12 minutes, until light and fluffy. Add the eggs one at a time, and beat until blended.

In a separate bowl, add the ammonia to the milk and mix well. Pour the milk into the mixer bowl and beat until blended.

In a small bowl, mix the baking soda into the orange juice until it starts to foam. Add it into the bowl of the mixer. Add the zest, salt, vanilla, and beat until blended.

Turn the mixer off and add the flour in increments, gently mixing it using a spatula. Remove the dough from the bowl and knead with your hands, on a working bench, until you have a smooth and malleable dough.

With a 1.75 inch (medium size) ice cream scoop make a small round and shape it into a strip. Fold it in half and twist.

Place the cookies onto the baking sheet, spaced ½ an inch apart.

Bake for 15-20 minutes.

While the first batch of cookies are being baked, prepare the second.

Notes: Baker's ammonia produces a lighter, crunchier crumb, and leaves none of the soapy-tasting residue of baking powder or baking soda.

You can easily find bakers' ammonia online or at Greek and Middle Eastern markets. If you can't find baking ammonia, you can substitute the same amount of commercial baking powder.

WorldwideGreeks.com **favorite**

Kourabiedes
Powdered Almond Shortbread Cookies

dessert

MAKES 24 COOKIES

INGREDIENTS

3 ½ oz slivered almonds (optional)

8oz unsalted butter, softened

½ cup powdered sugar sifted, plus about 1 pound extra for dusting

1 large egg yolk

1 teaspoon vanilla extract

2 tablespoons brandy (or cognac)

1 teaspoon of soda dissolved in the brandy

3 ⅓ cups plain flour, sifted with ¼ tsp baking powder

INSTRUCTIONS

Toast slivered almonds or pecans in a 350°F oven for 3-5 mins or until lightly golden and fragrant. Cool completely.

Line two baking sheets with parchment or silicone mats. Set aside.

In a stand mixer fitted with a paddle attachment, beat the butter and powdered sugar at medium speed, light and fluffy, about 20 min.

Slowly add the yolk, and vanilla mixing until combined.

Dissolve the soda in thae brandy and pour it directly into the mixer. Mix until combined.

Gradually add the flour and mix until combined (dough should be soft and pliable). Add slivered almonds, and mix on low until combined.

Portion cookie dough into a small cookie scoop (2 teaspoons) and roll into balls (about 1" wide).

Bake for 15-20 minutes or just until the bottoms are nice golden color. Do not over bake.

Cool cookies on sheet. Once cookies have cooled completely, Dust with powdered sugar.

Store at room temperature in an airtight container for a couple weeks. If freezing, do not dust with powdered sugar. Freeze for 1-2 months. Thaw out and dust in powdered sugar.

Notes: You can make the dough up to 48 hours in advance. Wrap in plastic wrap and store in a sealed container in the fridge. Bring up to room temperature a few hours before baking. The finished cookies will keep in an airtight container for up to 1 week.

WorldwideGreeks.com **favorite**

Melomakarona
Honey Cookies

dessert

MAKES 42 COOKIES

INGREDIENTS

SYRUP:

2 cups water

3 cups granulated sugar

¾ cup honey

2 cinnamon sticks

3 whole cloves

1 orange peel

½ teaspoon vanilla

2 teaspoons lemon juice

DOUGH:

1 cup sunflower oil

⅓ cup olive oil

¾ cup freshly squeezed orange juice (pulp removed)

Zest of 2 oranges

½ cup granulated sugar

¼ cup cognac

1 teaspoon cinnamon

¼ teaspoon cloves

1 teaspoon baking soda

1 teaspoon ammonia (or baking powder)

6¼ cups all-purpose flour

INSTRUCTIONS

For the syrup:
In a medium saucepan, combine the water, sugar, honey, cinnamon, cloves and the orange peel. Bring the mixture to a boil over medium-high heat, stirring occasionally. Reduce the heat to medium-low and simmer, stirring occasionally, until slightly thickened, about 5 minutes.

Remove from the heat and stir in the vanilla and lemon juice. Discard the orange peel. Position a rack in the center of the oven and preheat to 350°F. Line two baking sheets with parchment paper.

For the dough:
In a large bowl, whisk together the oils, orange juice, zest, sugar, cognac, cinnamon, cloves, baking soda and ammonia. Gradually add the flour, into the bowl and gently mix it using your hand. Mix it just until the dough comes together (30 seconds at the most). If you mix the dough longer the mixture will split or curdle.

With a 1.75 inch (medium size) ice cream scoop make a small round and shape it into an oval (like a small egg). Place the cookies on to the baking sheet, spaced 1 an inch apart.

Using a fork, lightly press the fork tines in the center of the cookie and create a cross hatch pattern. Place the cookies on to the baking sheet. Bake for 20-25 minutes. While the first batch of cookies are being baked, prepare the second. Makes around 42 cookies.

For the assembly:
Remove the baking pan from the oven. Remove the cinnamon sticks, orange peel, and cloves from the syrup. Place as many cookies into the saucepan as it can hold so that the syrup covers them. Let the cookies soak in the syrup, flipping them a couple of time to soak up the syrup on both sides. 1 minute for lightly soaked, 1 ½ - 2 minutes for moderately soaked, and over 2 minutes for very soaked.

Remove the cookies from the syrup and place them on a baking sheet from 4 hours to all night. Sprinkle chopped walnuts over the cookies and serve.

Store the cookies in a tightly covered container at room temperature for up to two weeks.

Tsoureki
Sweet Bread

dessert

MAKES 2 LOAVES

INGREDIENTS

4 cups bread flour

1 ½ packets dry yeast

⅔ cup sugar

¼ cup warm water

1 egg, room temperature

¼ cup orange juice, room temperature

⅔ teaspoon ground mahlepi spice

2 teaspoons vanilla extract

¼ teaspoon ground cardamom

¼ teaspoon ground mastic

½ cup warm milk

6 tablespoon unsalted butter, melted

1 egg

1 tablespoon milk

Slivered almonds, for sprinkling (optional)

INSTRUCTIONS

In the bowl of a stand mixer, whisk together 2-3 tablespoons of flour and yeast. Add 1 tablespoon sugar and the water. Stir gently to combine. Set it aside for 5 minutes, until it starts to froth, which means the yeast is active.

Fit a stand mixer with a dough hook attachment. Place the bowl on the mixer and add the rest of the flour in batches. Add the rest of the sugar, egg, orange juice, mahlepi, vanilla, cardamom, and mastic. Mix on low speed. Add the warm milk and then the melted butter.

Increase the speed to medium and mix for 10 minutes until the dough has come together. The dough will be soft and a little sticky.

Remove the dough from the mixer and place it in a lightly oiled bowl or plastic container and cover the top with plastic wrap. Press the plastic wrap directly against the surface of the dough to prevent a skin from forming. Let the dough rest for in a warm room for at least 2 hours, or until it doubles in size. Remove the dough and place it on a lightly floured surface. Use a scale and divide the dough into 6 equal parts and shape them into long ropes. Braid 3 ropes together to make 2 total braided loaves.

Line a baking sheet with parchment paper. Carefully place each braided loaf onto the baking sheet. Cover with a clean towel and let them sit in a warm spot for 45 minutes. Preheat oven to 350°F.

Meanwhile, in a small bowl, whisk together the egg and milk. When the loaves are ready to bake, using a pastry brush, gently brush them evenly with egg wash. Be careful that the egg doesn't puddle in the nooks of the braid as well as drip onto the sheet pan. Sprinkle with slivered almonds.

Bake for about 30-35 minutes, until the outside is golden brown and it sounds hollow when you tap the bottom. When ready, remove from the oven and place on a wire rack to let it cool.

Notes: You can find mahlepi online or at international grocery stores specializing in Greek or Mediterranean cuisine.

WorldwideGreeks.com **favorite**

Rizogalo
Oven Rice Pudding

dessert

SERVES 4-6

INGREDIENTS

- **1 cup arborio (short grain) rice**
- **2 ⅓ cups water**
- **3 eggs**
- **2 ⅓ cups milk**
- **⅓ cup sugar**
- **½ teaspoon salt**
- **2-inch lemon peel**
- **1 vanilla pod**
- **Cinnamon, to garnish**

INSTRUCTIONS

Place the rice and the water in a saucepan and wait until the water starts boiling. Lower the heat and cook for 15 minutes.

Place the eggs, milk, sugar and salt in a bowl, and then stir well until the sugar melts.

Add the boiled rice, mix well and empty the mixture into a 9x13-inch Pyrex dish. Bake in a preheated oven at 325°F for approximately 20 minutes until the mixture has set.

Remove the rice pudding from the oven, and set aside to cool for at least 10 minutes. Serve with a sprinkle of cinnamon.

Karydopita
Walnut Cake

dessert

**MAKES 12 LARGE
OR 24 SMALL PIECES**

INGREDIENTS

SYRUP:

- 4 cups water
- 4 cups sugar
- 1 cinnamon stick
- 1 orange peel

CAKE:

- 9 eggs, separated
- 9 tablespoons sugar
- 9 tablespoons walnuts, finely chopped
- 9 tablespoons Melba toast crumbs or plain breadcrumbs
- 1 teaspoon ground cinnamon
- ¼ tsp grounded clove
- Pinch of ground nutmeg
- Pinch of salt
- 2 teaspoon baking powder
- zest of 1 large orange
- 1 tablespoon vanilla extract
- ¼ cup cognac

INSTRUCTIONS

For the syrup: In a medium saucepan, combine the water, sugar, cinnamon, and the orange peel. Bring the mixture to a boil over medium-high heat, stirring occasionally. Reduce the heat to medium-low and simmer, stirring occasionally, until slightly thickened, about 8 minutes. Remove from the heat and discard the orange peel.

For the cake: Preheat the oven, to 350°F. Grease and flour a 9x13 inch baking pan.

In a bowl of a stand mixer fitted with a whisk attachment, beat the egg yolks with the sugar. Beat until the egg yolks are light and fluffy. About 8-9 minutes.

In a medium bowl, whisk together the walnuts, bread crumbs, cinnamon, nutmeg, cloves, salt, baking powder orange zest.

In a clean and dry large bowl, beat the egg whites until stiff.

Alternately, gently fold the dry ingredients and egg whites into the yolk mixture. Gently fold in the vanilla and cognac.

Scrape the batter into the prepared cake pan and smooth the top with a spatula.

Bake until the top of the cake is golden and a wooden skewer inserted in the center of the cake comes out clean, about 45 to 50 minutes.

Take the cake out of the oven. Using a ladle, drizzle a ladleful of the cold syrup all over the hot cake. Allow the cake to cool completely before serving, (at least 3 hours or overnight). Serve ideally with ice-cream or a Greek coffee.

Kormos
Greek Chocolate Log

dessert

SERVES 8-10

INGREDIENTS

2 packs (14 ounces) petit beurre biscuits

5 ounces unsalted butter, room temperature

1 ½ cups powdered sugar

½ cup cocoa powder

1 pinch salt

½ cup milk

¼ cup Cognac (or Liqueur of your choice)

INSTRUCTIONS

In a large bowl, break up the tea biscuits into small pieces. Set aside.
In a stand mixer fitted with a paddle attachment, mix together the butter, sugar, cocoa and salt until light and fluffy.

In a small bowl, mix the milk and cognac together. Drizzle the milk mixture over the biscuits while tossing with a wooden spoon in order to coat all the cookies. Allow the cookies to absorb and soften for 2 minutes.

Add the cookies to the butter mixture and stir until all the cookies have been coated. Place the mixture in the center of an 18-inch-long piece of parchment paper. Using a spatula, form the mixture into a log. Roll the log in the parchment paper and twist the ends to seal. Roll back and forth on a work surface a few times to make the log evenly round.

Refrigerate the log until firm, about 2-3 hours.

Slice cold using a knife that's been dipped in warm water. Serve with ice cream as an extra treat.

breakfast

Breakfast in Greece

Breakfast in Greece is one of the most nourishing meals of the day in all areas around the country. Coffee and tea are both common, and Greeks regularly enjoy pastry, bread, fruits, and other treats. It is also popular to accompany breakfast with eggs, Greek cheeses, olive oil, and olives.On a Greek breakfast table, you can find freshly baked bread, local honey, and feta. Kagiana is also a traditional egg and tomato dish which is particularly popular when tomatoes are in season.

For a lighter option, Greek Yogurt with Walnuts and Honey is a common choice. Greece is known for its variety of honey such as thyme honey, pine tree honey, or blossom honey (for more on honey see page 159). This is a filling, tasty, and nutritious breakfast that will fuel you for the day.

When on the go, Greeks turn to bakeries to pick up a variety of handheld pitas for breakfast. Pitas are created with phyllo and filled with various seasonal ingredients. Popular pitas include Tiropita (cheese), Hortopita (greens) Galaktoboureko (custard), Spanakopita (spinach), and others. Bakeries also serve other breakfast items such as Koulourakia (cookies), Koulouria (Greek bagels) and Loukoumades (Greek donuts).

To accompany breakfast, there are a variety of beverages. The most common breakfast beverage in Greece is coffee. Greek coffee is always freshly brewed, always strong, and prepared in many different ways. The most common types of coffee consumed in Greece are Traditional Greek Coffee and Frappe.

GREEK COFFEE
Preparation of the traditional Greek coffee uses a briki which is a small pot with a long handle. Freshly fine ground coffee beans are cooked in the briki with water and sugar (for those who like their coffee sweet). The coffee is cooked until it starts to boil and rise and then poured into a small coffee cup called a flitzani.

FRAPPE
Frappe is Greek iced coffee and is served as strong as it is cold. To prepare a frappe, instant coffee is mixed with a small amount of water and sugar (if desired), placed in a tall glass and mixed with a coffee frother until the mixture becomes stiff. Then ice, water and milk (if desired) is added to compete the coffee.

TEA & OTHER BEVERAGES
Many people prefer to start their day with tea rather than coffee. Greece has an abundance of locally grown herbal teas like mountain tea, chamomile and mint. Other beverages enjoyed for breakfast are freshly squeezed juices, warm milk and hot chocolate for kids.

In Greece, breakfast isn't considered the biggest meal of the day, but it is an important one. It's usually simple and designed to get the day started. The biggest meals in Greece usually take place later in the day.

Loukoumades
Honey Donuts

breakfast

MAKES 30-40 DONUTS

INGREDIENTS

DOUGH:

2 ¾ cups plain flour

1 packet of instant yeast

1 teaspoon baking powder

1 teaspoon salt

1 tablespoon honey

2 cups lukewarm water

Vegetable oil, for frying

SYRUP:

1 cup honey

1 tablespoon water

INSTRUCTIONS

In a large bowl, whisk together the flour, yeast, baking powder and salt. Add the honey, then slowly add the lukewarm water and stir to create a smooth batter.

Leave the dough in the bowl. Cover it with plastic wrap and place in a warm spot. Let rise until doubled in size, about 30 - 45 minutes.

Pour the oil to a depth of at least 3/4" deep in a heavy-bottomed 10" frying pan set over a burner. Heat the oil to 360°F. Take a teaspoon and first dip it in water to prevent the mixture from sticking.

Next, scoop a spoonful of mixture and drop it into the hot oil. The dough will sink but will quickly rise to the top. Do not overcrowd the pan.

Cook for 1 minute on each side or until puffed up and golden. Drain on kitchen towels, then transfer to a plate. Continue until all the batter has been used.

In a small pan, heat the honey and water until it is a thin, syrupy consistency. Remove from the heat and drizzle over the Loukoumades.Sprinkle cinnamon, walnuts on top and serve.

Notes: You can replace the syrup with a healthy drizzle of melted chocolate or Nutella.

WorldwideGreeks.com **favorite**

Bougatsa
Custard Pie with Phyllo

breakfast

MAKES 12 PIECES

INGREDIENTS

FILLING:

2 cups milk

2 cups cream

1 ¼ cups sugar

3 eggs

1 yolk

Pinch of salt

¾ cup fine semolina

1 tsp vanilla extract

¾ cup of melted butter, divided

1 box of phyllo dough, thawed

TOPPING:

Ground cinnamon

Powdered sugar

INSTRUCTIONS

Heat the milk, cream and half the sugar in a medium stainless-steel saucepan over medium-low heat. Bring the mixture to almost boiling, stirring until the sugar has dissolved. Remove from the heat.

Whisk the eggs and yolk with the remaining sugar in a heatproof bowl until well combined. Add the salt, semolina and whisk until smooth. While whisking constantly, add some of the hot milk mixture in a slow steady stream to the eggs to temper them. This keeps the eggs from turning to scrambled eggs when you add them to the simmering milk. Place the saucepan back on low-medium heat, and slowly pour the egg mixturein. Whisk constantly until the mixture thickens and you see bubbles reach the center of the saucepan.

Place a bowl in an ice bath. Remove the saucepan from the heat and strain through a fine strainer into the bowl. Stir in the vanilla extract and 3 tablespoons melted butter.

Brush a 9x13 ovenproof dish or baking pan with melted butter. Unroll the phyllo sheets and lay them flat. Cover with a damp cloth to prevent them from drying out.

Place 1 phyllo sheet off-center in the pan and let the edges hang over the sides. Brush the top sheet with butter taking care not to brush over the hanging sides.

Place another phyllo sheet on the other side, with overhanging edges. Brush the top sheet with butter taking care not to brush over the hanging sides. Continue on with this process until you have used half of the phyllo sheets.

Pour the filling into the pan and smooth out evenly. Fold the overhanging phyllo over the filling. Continue to layer the remaining phyllo sheets over the filling. Trim the overhang and push the edges into the sides so they disappear.

Brush the top with any remaining butter and sprinkle with a little water. Bake for 45 - 50 minutes, until the phyllo is golden brown.

Let the Bougatsa cool for at least 30 minutes and cut into 12 even pieces. Sprinkle with powdered sugar and cinnamon and serve warm or room temperature.

WorldwideGreeks.com **favorite**

Avga Tiganita
Fried Eggs

breakfast

SERVES 2-4

INGREDIENTS

¼ cup olive oil

4 eggs

Salt and black pepper, to taste

INSTRUCTIONS

Heat the oil in a medium pan over medium-high heat. When the olive oil starts simmering, approximately two minutes, crack the egg into a small bowl and slowly slide it into the pan. Repeat this one by one with the remaining eggs.

Slightly tilt the pan towards you, basting oil over the eggs repeatedly until the edges are crisp and golden brown and the yolk are slightly opaque, about 1 minute. Turn off the heat.

Using a slotted spatula transfer the eggs to plates. Season with salt and pepper and serve with a Koulouri or toast. To make this into a meal for lunch or dinner, serve with Tiganites Patates.

Kagiana
Eggs Cooked in Tomato Sauce

breakfast

SERVES 4-6

INGREDIENTS

- **¼ cup olive oil**
- **2 tomatoes, grated**
- **2 tablespoons canned tomato puree**
- **Salt and pepper, to taste**
- **5 large eggs , beaten**
- **1 cup crumbled feta cheese**
- **Chopped fresh parsley, to garnish**
- **Crusty bread for serving**

INSTRUCTIONS

In a large skillet, heat the olive oil over medium heat. Add the grated tomatoes and tomato puree. Add salt and pepper.

Cook for 20 minutes or until most of the juices have evaporate.

Add the beaten eggs and stir with a wooden spoon, so that the ingredients combine. Cover and cook until eggs have set.

Sprinkle with feta cheese. Serve with some Tiganites Patates and lots of fresh bread on the side.

Notes: For additional flavor, add ½ cup roasted red bell pepper drained and cut into strips along with tomato mixture.

Koulouri
Sesame Bread Rings

breakfast

MAKES 12 RINGS

INGREDIENTS

BREAD RINGS:

1 ⅔ cups water, warmed 95°F-115°F

1 ¾ teaspoons active dry yeast

3 tablespoons honey

2 cups all purpose flour

2 ¾ cups bread flour

1 ⅔ teaspoons kosher salt

2 tablespoons olive oil

SESAME TOPPING:

2 cups water

1 tablespoon honey

1 ½ cups sesame seeds

INSTRUCTIONS

In a small bowl, add ⅓ cup of water, yeast, 1 tablespoon of honey. Let it stand until foamy, about 5 minutes.

In a stand mixer fitted with the dough hook, combine the all purpose flour, bread flour, remaining 2 tablespoons honey, and the salt. With the mixer on low speed, pour in the yeast mixture, the remaining water and olive oil. Mix on medium speed for 7-8 minutes, until the dough forms into a soft ball and pulls away from the sides.

Lightly oil a large bowl and place the dough inside. Cover with plastic wrap and let the dough rise in a warm spot for about 55-60 minutes.

For the topping:
In a medium bowl, whisk together water and honey until honey dissolves. Pour the sesame seeds in a shallow bowl.

Preheat the oven to 400°F. Line 2 baking sheets with parchment paper. Turn the dough out onto a slightly oiled work surface and divide into 12 equal pieces. Roll out each piece of dough into an 11-inch rope.

Gently turn ends towards each other to form a circle or Koulouri. The rings should be roughly the same size.

Carefully dip each ring into the honey water and then into the sesame seeds. Place Koulouri on the baking sheet and bake for 15-20 minutes until golden brown. Serve with feta and tomatoes for a savory twist.

Notes: These rings are also known as Koulouri Thessalonikis

WorldwideGreeks.com **favorite**

Yiaourti me Karydia kai Meli
Yogurt with Walnuts and Honey

breakfast

SERVES 2-4

INGREDIENTS

- **2 ½ cups strained Greek yogurt**
- **¾ teaspoon vanilla extract**
- **⅔ cup walnuts, chopped**
- **½ cup honey**
- **Cinnamon powder**

INSTRUCTIONS

Preheat the oven to 350°F. Arrange the rack in the middle of the oven. Spread the walnuts in a single layer on a baking sheet and toast for 7-8 minutes or until golden and fragrant. Transfer the toasted walnuts to a bowl, add half of the honey and stir to coat.

Set aside to cool down for 2-3 minutes.

While the walnuts are cooling, mix together the Greek yogurt and vanilla extract in a bowl and then divide into four dessert bowls.

Drizzle the remaining honey over each bowl of yogurt. Spoon the honey-walnut mixture over the yogurt and sprinkle with cinnamon. Serve immediately or store in the fridge.

INDEX

INDEX

INDEX

INDEX

About the Authors

Pemi Kanavos sharing her recipes with some of the "Cooking Greek" village.

PEMI KANAVOS
Was born in Boston, Massachusetts and moved with her family to Athens, Greece when she was 8. Pam returned to Boston for college, earning a degree in Graphic design. Pam's love of cooking ran so deep that she decided to go back to school where she earned a second degree in Culinary Arts.

She has worked at various food establishments around Boston, wrote a column on a Greek cooking blog and taught Greek cooking classes for several years. Having moved back and forth between Boston and Athens, Pemi has now settled in Athens Greece with her husband and son.

This is her first cookbook. Follow Pemi on **WorldwideGreeks.com** and Instagram @PemiKanavos

TANYA STAMOULIS
Was born in Boston, Massachusetts, spent her summers in Greece and lived in Athens for a short time. She grew up in a strong Greek household that was always filled with family and friends sharing meals and enjoying each other's parea (company). Tanya's mom, Lena, could whip up a meal for 10 people on the spot at any given time without breaking a sweat. Watching her mom, her theia (aunt) Sonia and her yiayia (grandmother) Georgia make lavish meals in humble spaces, gather family and friends around the table and show their love through food, fostered her love of cooking and hosting.

Tanya and her husband Nick share a passion for all things Greek. They started **Worldwide Greeks**, as a space to celebrate, preserve and share their Greek heritage, culture and cuisine with the world. **WorldwideGreeks.com** offers a Greek cooking forum that has been used by over 500,000 Greek food lovers to discover the world of Greek cuisine.

Acknowledgements

Thank you to all who helped us through our first cookbook.

To our Greek village - we love you.

EFFIE KOUIROUKIDIS - For all the time you spent sifting through photos and lending us your creative eye, we thank you. We are forever grateful for your blunt and honest feedback and 24-hour free therapy.

MARIA-ELENA BISKINIS - Your attention to details and ever positive attitude helped us through our last days of editing. We are forever grateful to you for catching our "sweat bread" typo.

TINA CHRISTODOULEAS - You will always be our queen of grammar and favorite "edumakated" friend. We are sure there are at least 3 errors in this acknowledgement because we didn't show it to you ahead of time. Thank you for always being on board to support whatever we do.

Universal Conversion Chart

Oven Temperature Equivalents

250°F = 120°C
275°F = 135°C
300°F = 150°C
325°F = 160°C
350°F = 180°C
375°F = 190°C
400°F = 200°C
450°F = 230°C
475°F = 240°C

Measurement Equivalents

Measurements should always be level unless directed otherwise

⅛ teaspoon = 0.5 ml
¼ teaspoon = 1 ml
½ teaspoon = 2 ml
1 teaspoon = 5 ml
1 tablespoon = 3 teaspoons = ½ fluid oz = 15ml
2 tablespoon = 1/8 cup = 1fluid oz = 30 ml
4 tablespoon = ¼ cup = 2 fluid oz = 60 ml
5 ⅓ tablespoon = ⅓ cup = 3 fluid oz = 80 ml
8 tablespoon = ½ cup = 4 fluid oz = 120 ml
10 ⅔ tablespoon = ⅔ cup = 5 fluid oz = 160 ml
12 tablespoon = 3/4 cup = 6 fluid oz = 180 ml

Printed in Great Britain
by Amazon

2c215ce7-9af7-4caf-8f32-1e1075561eafR01